IN BUSINESS AND IN DATING

IN BUSINESS AND *in dating*

HOW TO NAVIGATE RELATIONSHIPS AND MAKE TOUGH DECISIONS LIKE A BOSS

ISBN: 979-8-9867157-0-4 (Paperback)

ISBN: 979-8-9867157-1-1 (E-book)

Bible references taken from the King James Version (KJV).

Petran Publishing.

Cover Design by Katarina Nskvsky.

Made and printed in the USA.

To all those who, along the way, have given me
an encouraging word or gesture.
Because of grace, this exists.

FOREWORD

One thing you can be sure of is that wisdom is the shortcut to success. When you learn to listen to those instructing you for your greater well-being, you'll find out that life gets a little easier; you avoid more losses and experience more wins. If you say you have a mentor, you ought to listen when they give you instructions or directions, as it is to your benefit. Mr. Boyd has always received advice very well, and as a result, he has also been a great steward of giving wise counsel. I know when he does seek me out, it's because he's already worked out most of the problem but is needing to add just a small part that is missing in order to solve his equation. He is always thinking, working, and planning in his mind—that's all he does, 24/7. He is actually a strategic genius.

So, when he asked me to write the foreword for *In Business and In Dating*, I said yes before he finished asking. I've known J.T. for a long time now and he is one of the most hardworking and dedicated men I know—he always has been. I myself am a very high energy man who is always on the move, and if there is someone I know that can do the same, it is him. While running errands with him one day, I asked, "When are you getting married?" He was not certain at the time. Though he was hardworking, as a mentor I could see that the amount of work he was putting in was not translating into a fruitful life. He owned a business near Beverly Hills, but his efforts were not producing all that they should have been. I knew that part of what was missing was stability in the area of relationships.

Finding the right partner is crucial to the success you will have in life, not just in your relationships but also in business. Through wisdom and guidance, Mr. Boyd made adjustments and changes that allowed him to marry a woman that was not only a wife but a life and purpose partner. To be honest with you, the moment that happened he started increasing instantly. The work actually reduced but the benefits increased. Shortly after, he sold the business, bought a house, and is now an executive leader at the fastest growing, multicultural, international non-profit, Revelation Church. Today, we have a plethora of business projects in development.

This book is one that everyone should read because it truly opens your eyes to understand walking with God, structuring your career and going after the dreams that God has given you, while also navigating relationships correctly, no matter how complicated they seem. Everything in life has a formula, and life is simplified if you understand the formula. *In Business and In Dating*, Mr. Boyd has truly cracked the code. I highly recommend it because there are many principles that are practical and immediately applicable to your life overall. It has even helped me, and I believe it will help those that will read it by helping them to be able to focus on what's important. Always remember that Boaz met Ruth when she was in a field. When you are in your field, what you desire or what God has for you will find you. This truly is eye opening and transforming, and I believe that once you read this book, you will agree.

Dr. Lovy L. Elias

Pastor & Founder of Revelation Church

Author, Mentor, Businessman

TABLE OF CONTENTS

PREFACE

In 1950, only 22 percent of American adults were single. Today, that number sits around 50.2 percent, which is about 124.6 million Americans. Back then, people got married younger and stayed married longer. Some would argue they did so either based on need, or because they didn't know any better. First of all, remember you're talking about your grandparents or parents at this point, so be respectful. All kidding aside, while there may be some basis for this argument, I would like to offer a different perspective. In fact, the greatest difference between relationships in our society today and the society back then is one word: simplicity. People were a lot simpler, as were the times they lived in.

Our present times can often appear 'simple' because of the great advancements in technology, but in reality, we have actually become greatly inundated with an abundance of options. The more options you have, the more choices you have to make; the more choices you have to make, the more energy you have to exert; the more energy you have to exert, the more you tend to want to conserve that energy; and when people conserve, they become way more selective and pickier with what they do with their now precious time. This causes us to think too hard about simple things, therefore making them more complicated. With meet and greet technology right at the fingertips of most people today, it creates an illusion that you have more time and can be more selective with choosing mates. And although this isn't completely incorrect, it just isn't completely accurate either.

Let's look at the 1950's again. In the fifties, high school graduates 'adulted' a lot sooner than the high school graduates of today. A few went to college, but most went either into the military or the workforce. Why? Well, there is an old adage that says, "if you don't work you don't eat!" Can you already see the trend? The high school graduates of that time embraced the options they had and made their decisions accordingly. When you give yourself fewer options to choose from you actually give yourself better chances at making the right decision. What is a right decision? Well, like the fifties, it's simple. A right decision is a decision you can live with. This means that although there could be another option of sorts if you really looked for one, you're ultimately deciding that it's not worth the time nor the effort. The sooner you can make a decision, the sooner you get where you need to go and do what you need to do. When you ask your parents or grandparents about their childhood and how they grew up, they always seem to be very confident about the things they share. Let me ask you; if I only gave you two options of anything, wouldn't it be easier to make a choice between those two versus two-hundred options? That is why our parents and grandparents did so much, why they got married young, had big families, and stayed married long— they knew what they wanted. The fewer choices you can give yourself the better your decision-making will be. It's up to you to learn how to turn the many into the few, and ultimately, into the one.

This book isn't about taking you back to the fifties; rather, it is about teaching you to simplify your life's choices. Every day, businesses have to make extremely tough decisions in order to thrive and in order to survive. One needs only to recall the year 2020 and how many boarded up. Some of those businesses weathered the storm and found their footing again, but many unfortunately did not and had to close. New businesses also emerged. Thinking like a business person is good, but thinking of yourself as a business is even better. You will understand this better in Chapter 1, and you will wish you knew this stuff sooner. I wish I did.

Had I known this information in my twenties, I'm certain my life would be different. I don't regret anything, however, because had my life been different, you wouldn't be getting this golden ticket that's about to change your single life as you know it. Before I met my wife, specifically from the time I was 16 until my mid-thirties, I averaged having a girlfriend every two years. That equates to 17 years of being in relationships; it was all I knew. I knew I was handsome but never subscribed to being a "player." Every woman I dated I treated extremely well and always desired to have a meaningful relationship with. However, most of them did not start on the right foundation, and the majority of the choices I made back then I would now consider toxic. I completely overlooked the options that would've been better for me. This isn't regret talking, it's simply self-reflection. There is not one aspect of my life I would change or go back and do differently.

I've loved and I've lost in dating, as in business. I've owned and ran businesses for over ten years, and there is one thought all sane business owners can rely on, which is, "This too shall pass." I remember my early days as a business owner and all the stressing I would do. After a couple of years in, I still didn't fully know what to expect. Each fiscal year either follows a set trend or makes a new one, good or bad, and sometimes you have to ride the wave of uncertainty all the way to the end before you know the outcome. I thought everything was supposed to go successfully, never preparing myself for anything else. One day, a business owner across the street from mine decided to stop in. He was probably 20-30 years my senior and had been in business for at least that long. We talked for a bit, but our conversation revolved around surface level stuff. Truthfully speaking, I was just proud to be a young black business owner at that point. As he turned to leave however, I felt the urge to ask him what he does when he is experiencing a bad month. He looked at me and said, "Sometimes you're going to have bad weeks, months and even years, but you just have to always believe things will get better and that the best days are ahead." Then he turned and walked out. I can honestly tell you that hearing those words from somebody who was more seasoned in business than I was uplifted my spirit and changed the course of every thought I had after that day.

I wrote this book to do the same for you. Where you are now and how you feel about your current dating or single life is about to shift. If you desire marriage, then you will get married.

What if you picked this book up just to learn a little more about business? Well, you will receive that too. The purpose of this book is to speak to those career focused individuals who seem to get in their own way when it comes to having a sustainable relationship that leads to marriage. If you think this book is about how to date just for the sake of dating, it's not. If that's what you're looking for, I advise that you return the book now and receive your full refund. However, if you can be honest with yourself and acknowledge that even though you might not have been in a relationship in a long time, at all, or have been in a string of failed relationships, yet you still desire to be married, then this book will guide you and show you how to get there.

In Business and Dating: How to navigate relationships and make tough decisions like a boss the goal is simple, and that is to get you to see yourself the same way a company sees itself in order to make the necessary decisions to achieve its goals. Business men and women have the understanding that the decisions they make are not personal. In fact, they've coined the phrase over the years, "It's not personal, it's just business," in order to fully condition you to not feel any type of way if in fact a business decision affects your life in a negative way. Ironically, our personal life is the exact opposite. It is, after all, called a personal life. If you were to always take things to heart, I can almost guarantee you that you would be keeping yourself from obtaining and achieving anything great. Sometimes it can be very hard not to take things personally, but ask yourself, "what has it benefited me to do so?" I really want you to think about that. I remember having a heart-breaking moment with a former girlfriend when I was 18 and carrying that pain with me well into my late twenties. At some point, after 10 years had passed, I called up my ex. We chatted, and all was well. Then I brought up the incident that I had been carrying around for the last 10 years. When I told her about it, do you know what she said? "I'm sorry, I don't even remember that." What?! So, you're telling me that the pain I had felt, that I allowed to stifle me for 10 years, was not even a memory to her?! That, my friends, is called life, and it is the reason we are here. I won't let anyone stifle your mind anymore, not even you. Begin to think of your life as a company. As we journey through this book, we are going to compare it with top performing companies, learn how they do it, and bring you to a place where you can navigate relationships, find the right partner, and ultimately, make tough decisions like a boss.

IN BUSINESS AND *in dating*

HOW TO NAVIGATE RELATIONSHIPS AND MAKE TOUGH DECISIONS LIKE A BOSS

CHAPTER 1

YOU ARE THE CEO OF YOUR COMPANY

(Knowing Your Self-Worth)

IN BUSINESS

Every year a list of the most profitable industrial corporations in the United States is compiled, called The Fortune 500. The companies listed are privately and publicly held, and are some of the largest companies in the world, ranked by their corresponding fiscal year. Fortune Magazine takes it even a step further; out of the 500, they highlight the Top 100 companies, or fewer. Although the companies listed all provide different services and products, there is one thing they all have in common. At the top of the ladder, steering the ship and navigating through the important decisions to further its goals, productivity and brand reach, is a Chief Executive Officer, better known as the CEO.

A CEO is the highest-ranking, most senior executive, corporate or administrative officer in a company. Their primary charge is to manage the organization by making major decisions, overseeing overall operations and resources, as well as being the main point of contact and the face of the company. A great CEO is vital to the success of a company.

Let's take a look at one of the most famous CEOs of our modern time, Steve Jobs. Steven Paul Jobs (February 24, 1955 – October 5, 2011) was born and raised in San Francisco, California and was put up for adoption. He attended Reed College in 1972 before dropping out that same year. In 1974 he traveled through India seeking enlightenment and studied Zen Buddhism. Then, in 1976, Jobs and his business partner, Steve Wozniak, cofounded Apple to sell Wozniak's Apple I personal computer. The two found great success and wealth a year later with one of the first mass-produced microcomputers, the Apple II. In 1979, Jobs saw the commercial potential of a mouse-driven, graphical user interface (GUI); this led to the development of the Apple Lisa. Though the Apple Lisa was deemed unsuccessful, it was followed by the breakthrough Macintosh in 1984, which became the first mass-produced computer with a GUI system. The Macintosh introduced the desktop publishing industry in 1985 with the addition of the first laser printer to feature vector graphics, the Apple LaserWriter.

Jobs was forced out of Apple in 1985 after a long power struggle with the company's board and its then-CEO John Sculley. That same year, Jobs took a few of Apple's members with him to found NeXT, a computer platform development company that specialized in computers for higher-education and business markets. In addition, he helped to develop the visual effects industry when he funded the computer graphics division of George Lucas's Lucasfilm in 1986. The new company was Pixar, which produced the first 3D computer animated feature film Toy Story (1995), and went on to become a major animation studio, producing over 20 films since then.

Jobs became CEO of Apple again in 1997, following Apple's acquisition of NeXT in 1996. He was largely responsible for helping revive Apple, which had been on the verge of bankruptcy. He worked closely with designer Jony Ive to develop a line of products that had larger cultural ramifications, beginning with the "Think different" advertising campaign in 1997 and leading to the iMac, iTunes, iTunes Store, Apple Store, iPod, iPhone, App Store, and the iPad. In 2001, the original Mac

OS was replaced with the completely new Mac OS X (now known as macOS), based on NeXT's NeXTSTEP platform, giving the OS a modern Unix-based foundation for the first time.

When Jobs died in 2011, he didn't just die as a man who had ideas that he let dance in his mind. He died an American business magnate, industrial designer, investor, and media proprietor. He was the chairman, chief executive officer (CEO), and co-founder of Apple Inc.; the chairman and majority shareholder of Pixar; a member of The Walt Disney Company's board of directors following its acquisition of Pixar; and the founder, chairman, and CEO of NeXT. He died a pioneer, not just of the personal computer revolution, but in the world of technology and business that we know today. Jobs' ideas and inventions became disruptors in our modern time whose effects will only continue to ripple through many years to come.

There is a reason Steve Jobs' story is so impactful. His legacy is not just that of the things he left behind, but also of how he lived his life. He lived life with the understanding that, "You are the key to your better future." He lived not being affected by things but affecting everything around him. He never stopped moving.

14

When he saw college wasn't for him, he didn't just drop out and work at a gas station—The End. Instead, he asked himself, "if college is not for me, then what is?" He put himself in search of what worked for him. It's clear one thing that was definitely working for him was his mind. He made sure his mind always sought solutions to the concerns he faced. After traveling and learning some key elements of life he and his friend founded a little company called Apple. The company had its successes and struggles, and when Apple forced him out, he started a company called NeXT. NeXT gave Jobs the environment he needed to create and be great without the shareholder pressures looming over him. There is nothing wasted in life or in business, everything can be used. It was the incorruptible developmental success he found there that ultimately led all roads back to Apple, except this time it was his time to truly call the shots. The rest, we know, is history.

Most people are so concerned with having a net worth that they aren't concerned with their self-worth. Clear self-worth is essential to obtaining massive net worth. Jobs understood his self-worth and knew when to separate from something that didn't contribute to it. He didn't bother himself with mere numbers to measure success but used progress as his ruler.

Whether people loved or hated him, he was all about moving forward. In business, he made all the moves that a great CEO would make.

WHO YOU ARE

Speaking of CEOs, guess what? You're one of them. Yes you! You are the next great CEO! This chapter is titled, "You are the CEO of your Company," because it is important to understand that you already run a company called, Your Life, Incorporated, for which you are in charge. Ultimately, you're in charge of your own happiness. The key to the better future you desire for yourself is YOU. Though you will employ many people along the way that will aid in making your happiness and goals a reality, it always will begin with you deciding what you want.

All successful companies have what they call core values or a mission statement, which outline the purpose and act as a compass that always points the leadership north, especially when difficult times come. The core values are a company's core authenticity and the reason why a brand is established. When you think of your life, who you are and the things you do are a product or service that can either increase or decrease the

16

awareness of your brand. Your brand is much like your character, personality, or what you are known for. Consider the pleasant things you've heard others say to describe you or your character. Now consider the not so pleasant things. Whether flattering or unflattering, that's your brand; it's what precedes you and what people go by. So then, ask yourself, how is your brand performing right now? Take a moment to really think about this and be honest with yourself.

While we can't control everything people say about us, we can control whether or not we are being consistent in displaying whatever our core authenticity is. As CEO of Your Life, Inc., establishing a good brand which you want to be known by is the TOP PRIORITY. It should matter to you whether or not your product is the best on the market, and like all top CEOs, you should want it to be. You can't be afraid to put in the hours required to take Your Life, Inc. to the levels that right now only exist in your imagination. The good news is that if you can in fact imagine where you want to be, then it indeed is possible to get there. It's important that you see your company as a Top Fortune 500. Better yet, make that a Top 50. You only get one life, so why not aim for the best?

Your company is extremely valuable, and the people you allow into it and the people you employ, will be equally important to its success and growth. You are the face of your company. If everything goes right, it all falls on you, and if everything goes wrong, it all still falls on you. In this position of CEO, there are no excuses and no one else to turn to, therefore your decisions have to be concrete and allow you to always move forward. One of the reasons I like to establish this link between your life and a company is because, as the adage says "the show must go on." Neither your life nor a company can afford to let any one person or thing slow or stop its progress. The only people you should want to be a part of Your Life, Inc. are those who want—and I repeat, *who want*—to better it. One of my core beliefs is that we should always strive to leave people, places and things better than we found them. Imagine if we all had this mentality. Moving forward, only give access to people with this mentality.

in dating

The value you place on your life is up to you. Others will perceive that value based on what you are producing. For example, if you look nice, dress nice, drive a nice car or live in a nice place, that will send a message to people. Take this note and never forget it: *everything you do sends a message to people.* It is true that some people can perceive the wrong message from you; however, if you are carrying yourself or operate as a high functioning individual who is intentional about the decisions you make, those around you will perceive you and your time as highly valuable. This will in turn also place you in high demand, and people will literally want to spend time, pick your brain and just be associated with you. When high value is established, however, it is equally important to note that compromise of that value can no longer be afforded. You can no longer sell yourself short or extend your stay in places you know it's time to move on from. The moment you compromise this, you, your time and what you produce will lose value to those it once appealed to. You don't have time to waste with people that simply don't value your time. The right partner will automatically understand this; so much so, you may find yourself less buried in your day and a lot more invested in their day to day. In doing so, however, you won't be losing anything. The keyword here is invested. Whatever you invest in the right partner helps you secure your value, and increases it even higher than it was before.

This process alone, although simple in text, can take some time. It takes time to find the right partner, someone that not only shares a similar vision or has even better plans for that vision, but someone whom you also desire to have around and go step by step with. Finding the right partner happens through a process called "interviewing," known in the relationship world as "dating." Like interviewing, dating is simply data collecting. You would be surprised how many people are not very good daters. While I don't necessarily think it's possible to be bad at dating, I do believe you can lack the tools to make you comfortable at it. This is why I simplified it in this way: dating is data collecting.

Too often, the stakes are made too high in people's minds when they go out on a date. One reason for this is the attempt to read a person's thoughts versus hearing their words and taking them at face value. If you just stay in the moment then the moment takes care of itself; but when your mind is wondering about things such as whether or not they like you, or you read too much into a statement they make, then the present moment will get away from you and more than likely you will seem a bit off your game. Obviously, the primary culprit is your emotions.

Learning to control our emotions is really the ultimate sign of maturity, not aging. When you go into a date, the best approach is to see it simply as two people sitting down to exchange information and hope to find something of mutual interest. This will help ease the angst or pressure to have a great date and allow it to flow better. So, just as an interview is data collecting, so is dating. It's that simple.

IN BUSINESS

Before you can begin your interview process, you have to be able to establish that you have an open position at your company. An open position is only realized when you take complete inventory of your strengths and weaknesses then determine you are ready to improve your weak areas. You need to ask yourself specific questions. What am I looking for? What do I need? Knowing this in advance protects you from making anxious decisions. In other words, just having a person who comes along and says they want the job won't be good enough. Figuring out if this person can not only do the job but also handle all the responsibilities that come with it is very vital to your company's success. Why? Because for every dollar and time you invest in a person that does not work out, there is no return on investment. Your money and time then are resources you'll never get back from this person, and out of these two the most important is time. Money can return to you, but time does not.

in dating

Another very important question to ask yourself when you're with someone that can save you a lot of time is, "Can I build with this person?" Honestly, there are several questions you could ask that would help you identify when you're in a good situation or need to leave a bad one. Another question to ask yourself is, "Do we have a good foundation?" When you meet someone, what are the circumstances in which you met, that is, what place, what reason, etc.? The foundation in which you are to build your relationship needs to be one that can stand the test of time and not be easily broken. It's even better when it's based on a shared or common interest. For example, I know a lot of folks who met while either volunteering in their local church, in charities or working at their job. You can change churches but your love for God most likely won't change. You can change charities but your heart toward that cause or other causes most likely won't change. You can change your job but your skill sets or overall interest in that occupation won't necessarily change. Any of these things can vary or change at any time, however the stronger the foundation you have, the stronger what you build with someone from that foundation can stand.

Let's prove it even further. We all know what a fling is right? A fling by definition is a short-lived period of enjoyment or wild behavior. In a fling, your personal value is reduced to instant gratification, a fix. It becomes the equivalent of a slot machine pull at a casino. Let's just say not all choices made during this time are good ones. Sure, there is excitement in the low-stakes, promise-of-thrill feeling you get, but eventually the low stakes become low interest and a big waste of time. Most of the time, we give ourselves permission to have them. We even call them *phases*, something we knowingly choose to enter and think we can knowingly stop at any point. Many times, however, we don't end the phase; the phase typically has its way with us then leaves us to collect the pieces. It's a sad but true reality that some people think of or only know flings as their acceptable way for building a foundation for a lasting relationship. This waste of time, even though you know you deserve better, causes you to choose between wanting the thrill of the fling again or wanting something everlasting. It becomes a battle. It becomes a rabbit hole and it can take its toll. Listen, I'm not here to judge. In fact, I've been there and tried it several times myself. You learn quickly, if not eventually, however, that flings rarely lead to the type of relationship you want to have. If you've picked up this book, then I'm confident you already know a thing or two about that, so instead of exploring the rabbit hole, we're going to stay above ground and climb a mountain instead.

CONCLUSION

(As you read below, replace every *'I think you're'* with *'I am'*.) The people you allow into your life and how they influence it is something you control. As the CEO of Your Life, Inc. you can't afford to make wild decisions, unless you see yourself as a startup. *I think you're* past that though. *I think you're* ready to do what Steve Jobs did. *I think you're* ready to leave behind what isn't for you in search for what is. *I think you're* ready for your thoughts to work for you and find solutions. *I think you're* ready to partner with the right person that can get your company producing great things. *I think you're* ready to keep thinking big and push for the best version of yourself and everything you touch. *I think you're* ready to see what being a high value individual can do for your life. No matter what you do, you can't do it alone. We all need help somewhere, and we will take a closer look at the interview process, aka dating, later. Before that, in the next chapter we will explore your company's market value (how others see you) and make sure we are who we think we are.

RECAP CHAPTER 1:

In Business: One of the most important people in an organization is the CEO. You are the CEO of Your Life, Inc. The CEO sets the tone for the company. Great CEOs have vision and are bold in their decision-making while being true to their core values. It's time to run your life like it is Your Life, Inc.

In Dating: If you know your value and self-worth, no one can waste your time ever again. The decisions you make for your growth and expansion are your top priority. Where your life is going and who you allow in your life is ultimately up to you.

THE APPLICATION:

- Create a mission statement for your life and identify your core values.
- Always remember you are in charge of your own happiness and future.
- Only give the people who want to better your life access to it.
- Seek solutions to concerns you have in order to keep moving forward.

- Evaluate your self-worth and give it a grade. Then, improve where needed.

CHAPTER 2

WHAT'S YOUR COMPANY'S

MARKET VALUE?

(How Others See Your Worth)

IN BUSINESS

In this chapter we are going to take a closer look at your company and examine its intrinsic value as well as its market value. Why is this necessary? Well, the answer is pretty simple. When you understand what your value is it allows you to set the proper expectation of what you can actually attract. What is intrinsic value? Intrinsic value is the measure of an asset with regard to its importance, worth or usefulness. Market Value, on the other hand, is the price an asset fetches in the marketplace or the present value an investment community gives to a particular business. This is essentially a component of how a valuation of a company is gathered.

In the last chapter we established that you are the CEO of a Fortune 500 company, Your Life, Inc. Don't lose sight of that, because how you see yourself is the most important determinant of how your confidence works and what is needed to be successful. Although we already have a vision of the company we're going to be, we need to also be able to acknowledge and examine the company we currently are and, most importantly, understand how others might see or value our company. What's the present value of your company? You don't get to determine that, unfortunately. At least not in the way you think. Your control comes in the many forms that create your company's value, culture, branding, quality in product or services, impact or need in the market. When it comes to the actual value, however, this is given by others. Does the way you run your company properly reflect your value and the markets?

MARKET VALUE

Market value is the price or amount a particular asset would get in the marketplace. It is the price the buyer is willing to pay the seller assuming both have knowledge of the asset's worth. It refers to the current or most recent quoted price for the market traded security or the value an investment community gives to a particular equity or business. It is also called Open Market Valuation or OMV. The market value is determined by the fluctuation of the supply and demand; it is not the value the seller offered, but rather the value the buyer is willing to pay. For example, if a person is selling their house for $750,000 but no one is willing to buy the house for more than $675,000 then that means the market value of the house is $675,000 and not the amount the seller or owner offered it for.

Market value can fluctuate greatly over a period of time and is substantially influenced by the business cycle. It plunges during bear markets that accompany recessions and rises during bull markets that happen during economic expansions. Market value is not market price, they usually differ. A market must meet certain requirements in order to be a fair market, one in which neither party involved is distressed. In other words, the buyer or investor doesn't have to buy or invest and the seller or business doesn't have to sell or seek funds. An example of a distressed seller is someone who is facing bankruptcy or a negative impact if they don't sell. The business and potential investor or buyer must have adequate information and market exposure. The business should have adequate time to search for the potential investor and the investor should have enough time to research and compare all the available alternatives. All terms are established through negotiation and mutual agreement rather than forced upon by either the potential investor or the business.

Determining market value, then, is important, and there are many methods to do it. We're going to look at one specific method, the comparable company method. The comparable company method is an analysis process which calculates the value of a company using the metrics of other businesses of similar size in the same industry with similar sales and profits. These are known as a peer group, and the information used should be recent in order to reflect up to date market conditions. Investors are then able to compare one company to its competitors on a relative basis. They do this by averaging together all the sale prices and using the average value as the beginning of an estimate of the market value of the company. Next, they use a multiplier such as EBITDA, a valuation ratio that measures a company's return on investment (ROI). In other words, because certain companies are in the same line of business or industry, thus having similar factors, then a ratio should be applicable for determining the value of one company by the value of another. So now that you have a brief understanding of how a company's value is determined, you may be wondering, "What does it have to do with dating?" I'm glad you asked.

in dating

First off, let's not kid ourselves. Our parents might think we're the best thing in the world, but we don't date our parents, and they are not our marketplace. Your marketplace is all the different environments in which dating happens. In these settings, your single life is on full display. Knowing your value, then, allows you to know what or who you can attract. Your value is your overall self-worth, which includes your standards and the high regard in which you see yourself. Never lose sight of your value, it's the most important factor affecting your confidence while in the marketplace; here, it will determine what's needed to be successful.

Your dating market value, on the other hand, is determined by how others see your popularity, age, relationship status, successes and attractiveness. Your popularity, how well you're known by others in different social environments, matters. Your age, whether you're too young to be thinking about a serious relationship or too old to still be single, matters. Is starting a family and having children still an option? Your singleness and the timing of it matters because it may cause more questions and be a red flag, or it can otherwise be completely understood. Are you fresh out of a relationship single or haven't been in one in 5 years or more single? Your successes matter because people want to know what exactly they are getting into when they meet you. They want to know how things are going for you financially. What do you do for a living? Are you just getting by or well taken care of? It's important to know as much as possible about a person up front, particularly in this area as it helps prepare for the proper mindset needed. And lastly, your attractiveness matters because depending on your level of attractiveness, some of the other areas will either be overlooked or highlighted. The more attractive you are the more you can usually 'get away' with. That's just how it is. The marketplace has determined this, not me. The less attractive you seem, the more it helps if your popularity, age, singleness and successes are top notch. Again, it is not me saying or determining this, but—say it with me—"the marketplace."

Essentially, these are the components of how valuations are gathered in dating; this is how the community of the singles and the dating will evaluate you. Although the marketplace factors in these elements at different ratios, its formula, once mastered, will not be undone by merely one thing. However, I personally believe your confidence is the disruptive factor in anything. In the last chapter we established that if you know your value and self-worth no one can waste your time ever again. This means that the decisions you make for your growth and expansion should be your top priority. When this is at the forefront of your mind it will naturally take care of a few of these areas we mentioned. So, ask yourself, "what is my present market value for dating?"

I suppose that answer can be subjective. What do you think a potential partner or candidate would say? Would they say you're a catch or would they want to throw you back? Literally, are you high on the desired by others meter or no one knows who you are? How much information about yourself have you presented or made available? How many single friends do you have and still hang out with? Do you make it a point to talk to people you've just met? Do you post pictures on social media? If so, what types of pictures and how many followers do you have? Do you have any blogs, vlogs, podcasts, or books? Oftentimes the willingness to date a person depends on how much information one has knowledge of. You can't attract what can't see you. Supply and demand are real equations in more things than you think. People want what they can't have or what everyone wants to have. For example, put a semi attractive person in an environment where they are the only gender of their kind and watch how the opposite sex will not only begin to relax their standards but also pursue said person. Their job would be at very minimum to not say anything to screw it up. Now imagine the reverse. Take an attractive person and put them in an environment where they are the only gender of their kind. Not only would they have many options to choose from, they would also settle in order to choose the best out of the possible selection.

This is the reason why most of us don't settle down in our twenties while the dating market is full of potential suitors. I recall back when I was in college, the female to male ratio was about 10 to 1. If you weren't a popular guy, it didn't matter too much; but if you were popular, then everyday was a party. Whether in college, the military, or the workforce, the combination of being young and bright-eyed causes us not to see great individuals when they are right in front of us. Even when we do see them, the distractions of life all around keep us from settling down with them. If that's your story too, then welcome. It didn't turn out all that bad for me because I have a smoking hot amazing wife who is the mother of my children. The point of all I'm saying is, if the demand and supply for you are high, it's a zoo! But if the demand and the supply for you are low, it's a paint drying marathon and it can feel like there are slim pickings. The sweet spot is when both the demand and supply are advantageous. Don't wait until a good one is hard to find; look hard and choose well when the market is full.

Never be too desperate or distressed in the marketplace, your market value will tank if you are. People can often 'smell' those who just want to be in a relationship. An example of a distressed person is someone who feels their clock is ticking and if they don't find someone soon, they won't be able to achieve certain things. The dating process should be just that—a process; one that would give ample time for two people to learn as much as they like at their own pace or a pace that has been established or agreed upon by both parties. All relationships are agreements. What does this mean? It means the terms upon which a relationship is established should be through mutual agreement rather than forced upon you by any potential candidates. In the next chapter, we will explore the hiring process (preparing to date) and make sure we're doing the right things to attract the right people to us.

RECAP CHAPTER 2:

In Business: Intrinsic value is the measure of an asset with regard to its importance, worth or usefulness. Market Value is the price an asset fetches in the marketplace or the present value an investment community gives to a particular business. The market value is determined by the fluctuation in the supply and demand. What's the present value of your company? Does the way you run your company properly reflect your value and the markets?

In Dating: Your marketplace is the environment in which dating happens. In these settings, your single life is on full display. Your market value, however, is determined by how others see your popularity, age, relationship status, successes, and attractiveness. Supply and demand is a real equation in more things than you think. People want what they can't have or what everyone wants to have. Don't wait until a good one is hard to find. Look hard and choose well when the market is full.

THE APPLICATION:

• Be fully aware of the market you're in and your value in it.

- Never appear too desperate, it tanks your value.

- Let your confidence (not arrogance) lead the way always.

- Always be truthful with yourself.

CHAPTER 3

THE HIRING PROCESS

(Preparing To Date)

Preparation (n.) – the action or process of making ready or being made ready for use or consideration.

IN BUSINESS

You've made some great decisions up until this point and your company has seen a lot of productivity, but, all of a sudden, things feel as if they've plateaued. You start to feel this insurmountable weight upon you to move things along, which then causes slight fatigue and no clear sense of what the next step is to get to your next goal. Every time you think of the tasks that lay ahead, air is let out, joy leaves you, stress rises and some anxiety sets in. Even when you're with a group of people somehow you still feel isolated in your woes. When you talk to colleagues you find yourself listening but in a mode of secretly comparing notes. As the CEO of Your Life, Inc. you wish you didn't feel this way but you do. You go back to the drawing board, review your core values, all seems right and you believe nothing has changed. So, what's the deal? It's simple; while it's true that you've accomplished great things on your own, it is now time for you to create something lasting and more meaningful for your company's survival. It's time to create an opening and start the hiring process to find the right partnership.

The hiring process is a process of preparation and preparation requires discipline. I've personally never known anyone who loves prepping for anything. However, if you ask high functioning executives what they think about preparation, you learn that it's very necessary in areas of top productivity. There are many key points to consider with this, one being time. First, you must allow an adequate time frame to compose yourself and take great inventory of Your Life, Inc.'s strengths and weaknesses. Like I stated before, you must know what you really need. Then, you must take adequate time for candidate exploration so you don't just rush to fill the role. This time that you take in your hiring preparation is the most vital, not just in finding the right person for the job but for you also.

Reflection can often produce great results. You have to be able to properly reflect over circumstances in order to know what or how to shift them. Ask yourself the hard questions to unlock the real answers within. These are some examples: Am I truly ready to share a part of my company with someone? This will show you if you're ok with giving up some control. What type of person do I want to hire? This will give you an opportunity to create your wish list. Are my choices and expectations realistic? This will cause you to examine your wish list over again and cancel any delusions that remain. I'm a believer that even though you can convince yourself of anything, you can't lie to yourself. Sit with your questions for a bit. If done correctly and given the proper time, you'll find the right answers that prepare you to meet the ideal candidate and produce great results. If done incorrectly, the wrong person will cost you unnecessary headaches, company resources and time, with time being the most difficult of these to recoup.

in dating

Perhaps you've heard the term "preparation is key." Well, the same is true in dating. A lot of people think they're ready to date because they've been single for a while. This type of thinking is actually proof that no preparation has been done.

You are in fact ready to date when you understand it has and serves a purpose. We will talk in depth about dating more in the next chapter. For now, let's take a closer look at what dating preparation for Your Life, Inc. entails.

Dating preparation is when reflection meets self-readiness. It's taking the time to ask yourself introspective questions. Do me a favor, think about where you are in life, what you do, where you live, how much money you make, and how satisfied you are with the way things are. Now ask yourself, "How did I get here?" I don't anticipate your answers will be negative, only that they will reveal there's been a pattern in your decisions somewhere. No matter how low or high on the mountain you are, the pattern in your decisions got you there. I do feel like that's another book, but let me connect the dots here. Oftentimes we end up where we do because we've accepted no guidance or see no flaw in our thinking and reasoning. Here is a secret, as long as you want to stay single there isn't a flaw in your thinking; but when you desire to share your life with another person you have to be willing to accept that your way of

44

thinking is now just another perspective. To put it plainly, if you want to be right all the time, stay single. If you, however, want a lasting and meaningful relationship, be someone who is open to reasoning with another person. You attract who you're ready for. I want you to attract the right partnership but do you know what you truly need?

The right partnership makes all the difference in the world. This is especially true when it seems you've carried the bulk of life's load by yourself. But are you ready for what you are asking for? Most people, perhaps those reading this book, decided at some point they were strong enough to attain a certain goal before allowing a partner in their lives. I've literally heard many men say, "I just want to have six-figures in my bank account before I make any permanent moves." That's noble, and anything is possible, but is it realistic? The average salary of males in the U.S. in 2019 was $38,461. I believe in success, I subscribe to it, and I know time is often its prerequisite.

Moving on to the women, I've also heard many women say, "I just want someone over six feet tall who makes a lot of money." Well, we just read the money statistics, so let's examine height stats. The average male height in the U.S. is 5 feet 9 inches. There are only about 14.5 percent of men over six feet tall in the US, and these numbers drop when you increase the territory to include the world. Again, anything is possible, however the question is, what are you most likely to encounter? The pattern in your thinking got you here. Many strong-minded and goal-oriented people unfortunately come to the end of their particular way of thinking when things don't pan out in their favor and they become anxious to just make a change. This point is called desperation, and we're now past that. If you're reading this book, that is not you. It's important to ask yourself questions and really think about the answers. Hopefully, you're now starting to see why dating preparation is so crucial. It takes your wish *list* and makes it rea*list*ic. And just to be clear, being realistic doesn't mean settling. It simply means taking practical and sensible steps to achieve your expectations or desires.

IN BUSINESS

Are you ready to make it known that there is an opening in Your Life, Inc. and fill that position with a quality candidate, someone who is ready to help take your company to its next level? When do you open the position for potential candidates? Like I said in the last chapter, an open position is only realized when you take a complete inventory of your strengths and weaknesses and determine you are now ready to strengthen those weaknesses. We often strengthen our weaknesses by hiring stronger people to take over that area. So, the answer is simple: it's when you're ready to let a small piece of your company go, not when you're distressed. By first being willing to let go of some control you're attracting the right partner to enter. The right partner will bring a certain peace to you.

I remember when I bought my first business, a smart phone repair shop in Los Angeles, California. I started from humble beginnings as a novice employee, worked for years learning the business and enjoying the people, became the store manager, then ultimately the owner. The original owners were two guys from Florida who went to high school together. In hindsight, I realized as partners both of them split different parts of the company's demands. They also split some nice profits. As time went on, after a few pay raises, I was told by the owners that they wanted to split the profits with me, offering me 20 percent to their 80 percent. My performance as store manager allowed them to worry less about the day-to-day operations and give more focus to their other businesses. As more time passed, I got

47

more profit share, then equal profit share until I was asked if I wanted to buy the place. The guys were so busy expanding locations in other areas they decided to reward me for the peace I produced. The point I'm making is, they could've kept all of their shares from the beginning but they were willing to let small portions of their company go in order to obtain their long-term goals as well as some peace. They could have said, "this is our company, we built this," and refused to relinquish control; instead, they saw me as the right partner to ultimately work with and sell their shares to. And for that, I am thankful because they gave me my first business owning experience.

That is what letting go looks like. It is focusing on the greater gain and making the necessary reductions and adjustments in order to obtain it. You no longer have to prove you have it all together or wing it, you just have to know there is help available to you when you're ready to receive it. When you take full inventory of things, you should know exactly what you're looking for. Ask yourself, "is what I am looking for really what I need?" Is what you're looking for going to make you a better you? Is your company going to improve? These answers should support your core authenticity.

REINVEST IN YOUR COMPANY

One of the things I like about this book is it gives you the opportunity to not only understand parallels but decide what company you see yourself as. Unfortunately, not everyone sees themselves as a Fortune 50 Company, and the truth is some of you are not. Some of you still just see yourself as a small business, and that's ok because those can grow. Let's take a quick look at small businesses.

A small business is a privately owned company that makes a certain amount of revenue each year. I believe the keyword here is private. Private things are usually associated with prideful things. It's true that all companies struggle all the time, but especially small businesses. They suffer in ways bigger companies don't because they usually have limited capital, and they don't reinvest enough of it back into their image or a new product line.

Typically, a small business that is losing customers could easily turn things around by doing a simple renovation of their image, logo or store front. These changes are known to attract new business all the time. However, what is often the case is they don't make those small investments, or when they do, they make them too late and end up losing out in the end. When I owned a brick-and-mortar business it fluctuated around the same earnings each month. The moment the décor and signage changed, business increased significantly. You might not be having a bad day, week, month or even year. Your Life, Inc. might just need to reinvest to attract the people you want to see. If you're unable to do this on your own, you might just need the right partner to come along and aid you. The right partner will be the investor your company needs.

in dating

I remember when I realized something in particular regarding my wife. We had been friends for about 5 years before we were married. Throughout those years, at times I was known to be very regimented. I owned my first business and liked things a certain way. I would show up to friendly gatherings a little after it would start and would disappear before it would end. While there, I would always enjoy myself but was never the last one to leave. My wife had the reputation of being the life-of-the-party-stay-until-it's-over-and-where-to-afterwards type. By the time we got married, however, we'd both completely changed.

I was getting very tired of being so disciplined about certain things and she was getting tired of flowing through things not knowing her next move to make. One day as I observed her, I saw just how disciplined she actually was about things. At that moment, I understood that her presence in my life was perfect timing. I needed a blow of fresh wind and she needed the structure of a mountain. She unknowingly began to strengthen me in my area of weaknesses and I began to do the same. You have to do the self-inventory to know what your strengths and weaknesses are and what you need. Until you do that, you're not ready to make any room for anyone in your life. Once you do this and know these answers then you're ready to start looking for candidates. I like to say it this way: as C.E.O. you are ready to find your B.A.E. (it's okay to laugh at that). We will cover choosing the right candidate in Chapter 4, but first, you have to become ready. Just as in business you have to reinvest in your company, so must you also do in dating.

LOOK READY, BE READY.

Dating Preparation requires more than just a mental shift, it also requires a physical one. Are you presenting yourself in the best way possible? This question is paramount in date prep. The saying, "you never get a second time to make a great first impression," speaks to this. You never know when an opportunity will present itself. Unless you have the rare ability to create opportunities wherever you go, you have to at least be able to seize them when they appear. In business and in dating that begins with a presentation. The way a thing is presented determines how it is perceived. Perception is based on the information that is presented for others to see. If you look good all the time it causes others to perceive you as someone important. Those terms are set by you and give you a lot of power in your preparation.

When was the last time you bought some new clothes and shoes? When was the last time you treated yourself to a spa day? When was the last time you groomed or primped yourself to perfection? These aren't the day or night of a date kind of questions I'm asking about but rather lifestyle questions. When you treat yourself well, others will treat you well too. When you carry yourself with confidence others will be drawn to that. There is this old football saying, "If you look good, you play good!" It's true. It's a lifestyle. Bring yourself to enter a new level. Find those who know how to do this already, watch them and ask questions. I have never seen a nice suit and a nice dress forsaken.

RECAP CHAPTER 3:

In Business: The hiring process is first a process of reflection. If you don't know what your company needs then you're wasting your time. Reflect on your strengths and weaknesses and look to hire according to what makes the weaknesses stronger. Reflection shows you where you need the most investment.

In Dating: Dating preparation is self-readiness. Your current standing in life is a result of every decision you've ever made. If you're not okay with what you see it's time to make an adjustment. It's time to do the work within to know what you're ready for. Be open to trying new things to get different results. Make room for someone to enter your life before they get there. Since first impressions are powerful, take the time to take care of yourself and make it a lifestyle.

THE APPLICATION:

- Understand that preparation is a choice.
- Identify and learn exactly what you need.
- Ask yourself the hard questions to unlock real solutions in the areas you need.

- Always remember you attract who you are ready for.

CHAPTER 4

CANDIDATE SELECTION FOR THE INTERVIEW

(Choosing Who To Date)

Intentionality – the fact of being deliberate or purposeful; having a plan or aim.

IN BUSINESS

A few years ago, I was looking to fill a position because an assistant manager, a talented actor and musician, decided to leave in order to actively pursue his dreams. I supported his decision completely. I firmly believe that when people want to go, they've made their choice and should be permitted to do so. Don't hold them back and don't try to convince them otherwise, it's just not worth it. As I began calling around to schedule interviews, he and I would chat in between calls. I told him that one of the things I loved about being in a position to hire someone was that I could literally change a person's life. A person could go from despair to hope to faith to reaping, with just one call. That's when it hit me—when you're in a position to hire, the candidate must also want the job! The same is true in life—in your life—especially regarding relationships.

In other words, you're always the one in charge of making management decisions as it pertains to Your Life, Inc. The only responsibility you have is what you've been given authority over. When you are entrusted with a position of authority, it usually signifies that you have at some point proven that you can handle an increased level of responsibility efficiently. Having said that, I had to remind myself that the same is true for selecting candidates to interview or "choosing who to date."

If you were to set up an interview with a candidate because there was an opening in Your life, Inc., and if said candidate was not interested, as a boss, you are not to still pursue the candidate. Why? Because, if you have to convince someone of your worth once, they most likely will have to be convinced over and over again. So, what do you do? Do you move on? Absolutely! You move on, until you find the right candidate, someone who is the best fit for the needs of the business, that is, you and your purpose. Thinking about it this way really creates a non-negotiable standard that always keeps your company,

Your Life, Inc. moving forward. If you have a position open in your company, all you can do is let it be known. When you see a candidate that you want but who, once you put your offer out there, is not interested, you move on; anything else would be unhealthy for your company. This is why intentionality is one of the main keys that unlocks the whole process to work in your favor. When you are intentional about taking your company to the next level, all decisions matter, but no decision is as important as who partners with you in order to do so.

in dating

The same is true with choosing who to date. When you are intentional about taking your life to the next level, all decisions matter, but no decision is as important as the person you choose to enter a relationship with. Intentionality reveals terms and conditions, and helps people know what they are signing up for. Let us consider what being intentional looks like for men and women in dating.

For men, being intentional means knowing what you are looking for in a partner, and having a clear timeframe of marriage which you're willing to communicate to the right person in order to begin dating. An example of this is, if you are a man, letting a woman know upfront that you're actively seeking companionship and looking to get married within the next 1-2 years. When the right woman hears that, if she's interested, she will not only see you as a man with a plan but also be more willing to align herself with you and your vision. For women, being intentional mainly involves being socially visible, open-minded and most importantly, approachable. Socially visible simply means that you, as a woman, are out in places where people meet and are not just sitting at home waiting for someone to knock on your door. To be open-minded doesn't mean settling, but rather the willingness to put aside every Hollywood or Disney fantasy regarding relationships so that you are now open to meeting a man who may not be like what you've envisioned all your life. To be approachable is to be friendly or easy to talk to.

For both parties then, it definitely means putting yourself in environments that increase your chances for encounters with the right people to happen. It also helps, when you're in these certain environments, to know what you're looking for, be socially visible and approachable, and have a clear timeframe you'd be willing to communicate with the right person if sparks fly. Do this, and you will have created an opportunity for relationship success.

CULTIVATING GOOD RELATIONSHIPS

Cultivating good relationships—personal or business—is the key to the doors you'll need to open up opportunities in your future. Rarely will you ever come to a door in life that a previous relationship did not help you to get to. This is why the phrase "don't burn bridges" is a principle to live by; you never know when you may have encountered a person in one stage of your life that will help you in a later stage. The person you could not stand in high school or college may be the contact you need to assist you in getting to your next opportunity. Having this mentality will not only help keep you open-minded to the potential business relationships you can form, but it will also make you very intentional about the potential companions you entertain.

To put it more plainly, when you become open-minded it will cause you to better distinguish between clear possibilities and clear liabilities. This is what the interview or the date is all about. It's a face-to-face meeting where dialogue and data will be exchanged, either virtually or in-person. At the conclusion of that meeting, there may be hope for a second round of communication. Should that happen and if all goes well there, then perhaps a third round is scheduled at a later date. The third round is the most crucial—it usually aims to validate whether the thoughts and notes from the second-round stand, good or bad, or if there is something that was overlooked. Assuming the third round is successful, which usually happens as a result of the time that has been invested thus far, it is a fair consideration for conversations to persist and for both parties to be interested in potentially extending their time together by a mutual agreement. In case you missed the dating reference, by the third date, it is fair to assume the other person either will ask to continue seeing you or communicate otherwise, because by that point and time it has to be believed that enough information was gathered in order to form that decision.

How does this happen? For starters, focusing on clear possibilities helps you to create a solution-oriented mindset. This means you will only focus on clear paths to your desired outcome instead of the problem itself. As a result, it shouldn't take long to know if someone is for you or not. While it is a process, when questions are asked during an interview, how a person behaves, responds or applies their answer to the question becomes just as important as the answer itself. When dating, how a person behaves on the date, how they respond to and treat you, and how they react to different social environments should be enough information for you, with an intentional mindset, to know if they are worth extending your time together by mutual agreement or not. It is important that you stay focused during this very crucial process. The success of Your Life, Inc. depends on it. Now that we've covered that, let's go on a date. In the next chapter we'll explore the interview and dating process even further.

RECAP CHAPTER 4:

In Business: To be in a hiring position means you have a perceived degree of power. When you are conducting interviews for Your Life, Inc. you have power. Use it, and assess circumstances properly. Is this candidate worth your time and resources? There are various types of candidates out there, and you should be very aware of types you're going to be running into.

In Dating: Intentionality serves as the greatest component in finding the right partner. It introduces terms and conditions. The more upfront you can be, the better. Once the terms are put on the table, they're either accepted or declined. Both are good because it's information you can use instead of trying to read someone's mind.

THE APPLICATION:

- Always be intentional with the decisions you make concerning every component of your life.
- Don't pursue those not interested in you.

- Evaluate and distinguish between what are clear possibilities versus liabilities.

CHAPTER 5

THE INTERVIEW

(Dating)

IN BUSINESS

I want to tell you a secret. Seeing as we're in Chapter 5, I believe you're ready to be granted some exclusive access behind the curtain. What I am about to tell you is something all bosses know and especially feel. This little secret could make all the difference in your understanding of this chapter. Are you ready? Okay, here goes...listen carefully, "No one likes the interviewing process." Find me 10 people with hiring power, and I guarantee you will have found 10 people who'd rather be doing other things. It's not because they don't like seeing lives changed, that's actually the best part.

It's because if you find yourself preparing to conduct an interview or be interviewed, it means a role needs to be filled, often because someone was either fired or quit unexpectedly. For an interviewer, it means someone in your company that you once trusted or trained to take care of specific duties and tasks is no longer there. Who likes it when that stuff happens? Furthermore, there are usually no guarantees that you will find what you are looking for within the timeframe you expect. A quick hire replacement usually doesn't work out either. Thus, the interruption from the other things you could be doing is a costly one. You could be executing and facilitating business deals yet a series of drawn-out interviews in order to potentially find the right candidate has your focus. In large corporations, the CEO isn't handling these kinds of things, but in Your Life, Inc. you are. How are you readying your company? Are you considered one of the top places to work? Are your offices clean and files organized? Is the accounting in order? Is your property well maintained? No employer wants to repeat this process over and over. Your goal is to find someone who wants to be a part of your company and go from there.

in dating

Interviewing is the fraternal twin to dating. No one likes dating, especially when you're in a place where you have to date. What dating truly is and isn't needs to be explored a little bit further. Although you could say it's subjective, in our modern times

68

many have turned dating into this unintentional time-wasting thing you do until one or both parties get tired of their current status and apply pressure on the other to change the narrative. This makes the passage of time the main catalyst for what happens next in the relationship instead of the most important driver, intentionality. As stated above, find me 10 people wanting to be in a seriously committed relationship and you will find those same 10 are probably over the dating scene.

Finding the right partner to do life with can be an arduous task, especially if your singleness isn't being spent reflecting upon and preparing yourself for your next opportunity. To put it plainly, and it cannot be said enough: if you're not being intentional about your next relationship opportunity then you're not being intentional about your life. I'm not saying it's wrong to be single because there are some definite advantages to it, but the reality is, if you've picked up this book, then you're probably not interested in being single. What you prepare for determines your probability and sustainability when the opportunity comes. For example, if you ever played team sports you may remember there was always a depth chart at each position. Usually, the way most coaches operate is that the starter is the best, behind the starter is the second best, and so on and so forth. In order for anyone number 2 or below on the depth chart to get that number 1 spot, a series of events would have to happen in order to make that position open. Regardless of what causes that event, if the number 2 hasn't mentally and physically prepared for that opportunity when it is presented then it will pass them by and go to the player who is. The most prepared person will always get the job when opportunity knocks on their door. So, how are you preparing for your next dating opportunity? Do you love yourself? Have you let go of the past? Have you reconnected with your interests? Are you being open-minded? Are you fun to be around? Have you been taking care of yourself? If you have incomplete answers, it won't attract the right people. What I am saying is, it's time to evaluate your singleness and see how and why you got there. Reflect on what your trusted family or friends have told you about yourself over the years, good, bad or indifferent, to see if there are areas of improvement you can address. While life is about so much more than these things, these things can enhance your life if properly assessed and applied.

IN BUSINESS

It's important that you see Your Life, Inc. as an always evolving entity. Remember in the beginning of the book where I mentioned having a mission statement or core values? The reason for that is because they are your roots. They provide you with balance, which is necessary for growth. It is much like trees; before they sprout up to face the harsh conditions of the awaiting world their roots have to set deep in the ground. You have to know your core values to know what you are staying true to and what to change. While a company must always be open and looking to be innovative, so as not to become set in their ways, by knowing its core values it will better assess risks for opportunity. It doesn't matter how old Your Life, Inc., is, you must be open to evolving in order to be successful.

TOO LATE FEE

When I was in high school, I landed what is to date probably the best, most enjoyable job in the world to me. While most teens get jobs working at camps, water parks, and fast-food restaurants, which I also did, the most exciting job was when I got to work for Blockbuster Video. If you don't know what that is, it was a magical place that existed before the advent of online streaming. Movie lovers could go there, find the latest movie release or favorite movie, rent it for a few days, return it, and repeat the process. I loved that job! I loved it so much that when I went off to college, I came back home to work there for the summer. Those were the days. Anyway, everyone thought Blockbuster was here to stay. After all, when movies left the theaters, they had to go somewhere, right? And with a record high of 9,000 locations at one point, the business model seemed fool proof. Well, at the time of writing this book, there is currently only 1 location in the entire world left, in Bend, Oregon. The Blockbuster Story has become a highly studied business case. How did something so big and so successful fail to exist in the current time as we know it? I mean, it started with VHS rentals and transitioned to DVD & Blu-ray, which was evidence enough that there was someone at the top who understood the market and change in times. Although a few great changes were made, it wasn't enough. They weren't prepared for the great wave that was coming of online streaming—more specifically, Netflix. If you study this scenario in depth, you will learn that Blockbuster had chances to not only compete but actually acquire Netflix. Netflix essentially could've become Blockbuster's online business. Unfortunately, a lot of the decisions made by the CEO were too little too late.

Although I can talk about this case study in greater detail, and I actually encourage you to study it, I want to simply focus on this point, the greatest lesson we can draw from it: if you can remain open to learning, growing and evolving, then you are staying prepared and making room for great things to happen to Your Life, Inc.

in dating

Dating the wrong people or being single for long periods of time can cause us to take circumstantial information that we learn and make them become our life standards. In other words, what or who we expose ourselves to develops our preference of types of companions, habits or expectations, and makes them our norm. If we find nothing wrong with the past choices we've made, then we won't see the right ones to make. If the reflection time is used as preparation for what's next, as we've established, then we will naturally make better choices than we have in the past. If it is not, then it can definitely work against us making the progress we want to see in this specific area of our lives. This is how you end up in another go-nowhere relationship with the exact same or similar type of person each time. The problem becomes that we've accepted the past and its information as the best-case scenario instead of challenging it. It's hard to challenge things without the proper know-how. We seldom re-examine the stockpile of information or data we've acquired during that time of bad relationship or singleness and ask simple questions like, "What can I improve on? What can I change? What does the current dating scene look like? What books can I read to learn more about relationships? Who can I talk to for mentorship? Who can help me understand a different perspective?" What I'm saying is, the information you feed yourself becomes what your actions pull from. So, then, at this point, do you know what you're looking for? Do you know what you're willing to consider? Can you offer the right package for the person that you want? Are you willing to take the necessary time it takes to develop, grow and attract the right fit? Are you being realistic?

IN BUSINESS

The questions you ask in an interview are supposed to give you some insight into the person you're potentially looking to hire.

However, interview questions over the years have become pretty standardized, and consequently, so have the answers. The answers to interview questions have become too "I-want-to-impress" that opportunities are being missed. Take note of what I'm about to say here because this is crucial for you to grasp: what you say during an interview, and how you answer questions, is verbal currency. You might be wondering, what is verbal currency? Verbal currency are words that can be exchanged for valuable actions. If your words are empty, so are your actions. Experienced interviewers can tell the difference between a people-pleasing answer and one with substance.

Here are some of the most common interview questions and their meanings:

- Tell me about yourself. (Intentionally vague, but gives candidates an opportunity to make themselves seem interesting.)

- What is your greatest strength? (This gives the opportunity to display confidence.)

- What is your greatest weakness? (This gives the opportunity to display what they've learned through experience as well as humility—because we all have weaknesses. There is no such thing as, "I don't have any weaknesses.")

- Why should we hire you? (If a candidate has done research on the position and the company, they should be able to knock this question out of the park; there is clearly a need to fill and the candidate's skill set is what they are looking for.)

- What's something positive your boss would say about you? (Translation: Do you follow authority well? Are you a team player? Do you take initiative? Are you growing with this role?) - What are your salary expectations? (How you sell this is a real test of confidence and knowing your worth, as well as being grounded.)

- Why are you leaving your current role? (Allow self-reflection and self-worth to lead this answer. Leaving something behind isn't always based on negative reasons; many times, it is for growth purposes.)

- Why do you want this job? (Again, doing your research on the company, your confidence, your self-reflection and self-worth should lead you in answering this question, which is really asking, Are we just another job to you?)

- What interests you about this position? (Tell something, preferably a compliment to the company, that simultaneously makes them feel special while setting you apart from other candidates.)

- What are your future goals? (Are you a waste of time? Are you worth our investment in you? Express how your mind works and how you see yourself.)

- Describe a difficult work situation and how you overcame it (Are you a problem solver? Are you a leader? Do you take initiative on your own or do you need your hand held?)

What most people don't know or feel comfortable with is that you are supposed to have questions for the hiring company as well. This is a small fact that is often overlooked. You're supposed to interview them as they are interviewing you; this shows your value.

in dating

Much like first interviews, or any subsequent one, your first date or dates can be full of pressure. The line of questioning is basically the same, and usually clues aren't given to signal whether the answers were adequate enough until well after the fact. Some people believe they're supposed to go on dates and wing it. While I agree that you should definitely go with the flow, it's also totally okay and beneficial to be prepared. If you're the initiator, plan the date and know what you're going to be doing. Call ahead, make the reservations, choose an outfit that boosts your confidence and maybe have a few questions prepared to keep things flowing if you need them.

Here are some of the most common date questions that you can ask creatively, or if asked to you, you can knock the answers out of the park.

- Why are you single? (It's a trap! No, I'm joking. This allows you to showcase true maturity, humility, and accountability.)
- What makes you unique? (This is your standard show-me-your-confidence question. Let your personality show. What types of things do you find funny? Share them.)
- What are some random fun facts about you? (While this one should be easy, try not to make it bland. Let your personality

and quirks show a bit. Remember, we're past the I-want-to impress mode of thought and in the let-me-show-my-value stage.)

- What is something you want to learn or wish you were better at? (You might not be where you want to be or even know exactly how to get there, but a question like this, if answered properly, is an opportunity to show your humility and tenacity at the same time.)

- Would you rather *this* or *that*? (This is a great type of question if you're clever. Such questions can give excitement to what could be two boring options. Plus, you can scale these up or down to find out more about how a person thinks.)

- Know any good jokes? (If you're asking this question, hopefully things are still going well. Just be naturally funny or tell good jokes and let the other person return the gesture if they can.)

- What's your favorite place on earth? (Explore your creativity here. I'm not saying don't give an obvious answer, but I'm saying don't be boring in how you give any answer.)

- Who are the special people in your life? (Here is another easy homerun, if answered properly. You might want to add, after the answer: "I wonder if I will be one of your special people one day." This question is giving you an opportunity to shape how you honor and value the people closest to you. One day it could be your date that you're talking about, so really take your time and give meaningful answers.)

- What's been your favorite vacation? (Let's be honest, have you really traveled the world and seen all the places you've wanted to see? If the answer is no, then your favorite vacation so far might be weak, but say it anyway and throw in there your dream travel destination. If the answer is yes, then paint very vivid imagery as to why it was your favorite.)

- What are you currently obsessed with? (A very basic but brilliant question. In this you can dive into the real usage of time of a person. Their interests can reveal a lot to you.)

- What are you most passionate about? (Similar to the previous question, but this moves things beyond a certain moment and into more of a life cause. What really drives and motivates you?)

- Are you a morning person or a night owl? (Not to be overlooked, because this is a key question. Are we in sync? Can we get in sync? People are different, therefore knowing as much about a person as you can helps manage your expectations. If they tell you something about themselves in the beginning, don't expect it to change, respect the differences, and adjust where possible.)

I hope you've learned something about the different questions you can ask and what they secretly mean. Obviously, the intention is to help you win, not manipulate people. I wouldn't even waste time trying to do that because in life you truly do reap what you sow. Hopefully, with these questions and the many others you may add, you can condition yourself to perform the way you intend to, and not the way you didn't intend.

I have some great news: you are about halfway through the book! Now, it's time to dive even deeper. In the chapters ahead, I'm going to help you uncover the 4 main types of candidates to look out for, and the pros and cons of each one. By the end, you will know exactly where your trouble spots have been and what you need to do about them. These candidates happen to be the four types of people you should look out for in dating as well. They are the Easy Hire (Eager Daters), the Uninterested (Time

Wasters), the Top Recruits (The Ones Everybody Wants), and the Game Changers (God's Gift to Someone).

RECAP CHAPTER 5:

In Business: No one likes interviewing. It just has to be done because something opened up. Interviewing or how you interview is a vital component to your company's future success. It gives you the opportunity to find serious people who mean business. The things you discover during an interview aren't just words on a sheet but verbal currency, words that can be exchanged for valuable actions. Your core values can give you indicators needed to know when it's time to evolve in your thinking a bit.

In Dating: No one likes dating. This just has to be done because there's an opening in your life. Whether you're looking for someone or someone left. Whether you or they did the breaking up, there's an opening. It is however an evolutionary practice. If prior to dating you haven't reflected on things and can honestly track how you got there then you're not ready to start. Dating involves preparation and intentionality. Always be open to going with the flow but don't be afraid to have some things pre-planned.

THE APPLICATION:

- Make sure you look good, maintaining a clean and kept appearance. Look professional.

- Make sure you're in social settings that allow for opportunities to meet someone great.

- Make sure you're approachable, that your demeanor is kind and friendly enough to have conversations with those that approach you.

- Be prepared. The most prepared person will get the job when opportunity knocks.

- Always stay open to learning, growing, and evolving in areas you want to improve.

- Ask the right questions to help you better understand the person you're with.

- Don't expect a person to change; respect differences and adjust where possible.

CHAPTER 6

THE EASY HIRE

(Eager Daters)

IN BUSINESS

When Your Life, Inc. hasn't taken proper inventory of its liabilities or staffing needs, filling an opening can be done hastily. The focus becomes more on filling a position than finding the right person for the position. Unfortunately, anything done in haste usually yields less than desirable results. Sometimes you just have to do what you have to do, but you eventually learn that the time invested wasn't enough and you'll have to repeat the process of filling the position again. The reason this happens is because of Easy Hires. If your company doesn't plan its time and do its due diligence during the hiring process to qualify the right candidates, then an easy hire can slip through your doors. You might be asking, what is an easy hire?

An easy hire is a person, who at the time of meeting them, is unemployed often for periods of 6 months to a year, or even more, and seems very eager to land a job. So, when their résumé lands across your desk when you are in a desperate state due to a lack of organization, as mentioned above, causing the hasty moves, you will call them in for an interview. And because they are also desperate—but mask it as enthusiasm—their eagerness and "yes's" can seem like the answer to your hiring prayers. The lack of due diligence or extensive interviewing process, checking references, feedback from others, etc. can cause you to give a green light to a person that honestly and truly just wants the benefits. Their vision for your company won't be how they can help you produce results, only what the company can produce for them. These people will get on board, learn your system, do enough to make it past the 30, 60, or 90-day training period, then will stop actively contributing. This then forces you to have to fire them—that's if they don't quit first—and starts your hiring process all over again. In most cases they will prefer you to fire them because they can then apply for unemployment and coast once more until they have to get another job. Hopefully your company is made better from the experience and you learn what not to do again, which is always the goal.

You win or you learn. Notwithstanding, the experience can still leave you just a little more exhausted than before.

in dating

When it comes to dating, if you haven't taken proper inventory of your life, wellness, baggage, true needs or true self-worth, you will allow a "desperate-to-enter-a-relationship" type into your life. These will be people who most likely haven't been in a romantic relationship in the last 6 months to a year, or more. Their main desire or objective is to just get into a relationship by any means. For them, a relationship represents a welcome distraction and excuse to not pursue their personal goals. Their desperation will also be masked as enthusiasm; being overly complimentary, overly charming, overly accommodating and even a little clingy. They may share their deep feelings for you very early as well. Don't get me wrong, these aren't bad people. However, what they do comes from a place of need versus a place of generous giving, thus it's not truly authentic and will only last temporarily. When dating a person like this, you will find that convenience is their main concern.

Please hear me. When dating a person like this, you will find that their convenience is their top priority. They will do enough to make the first 30, 60 or even 90 days seem promising and even magical, but later you will realize that it has been an illusion the whole time. At first it may take a while to notice, the reason being that you don't truly know *what* you need, just that you have a need. It will initially feel like a void has been filled, but as time goes on, not only do you realize the need is still there, but your new person isn't helping or may even be the cause of new problems.

When it comes to making decisions, most of the time, we usually know what we need to do. The problem is that we override our decisions and the ability to make them by factoring in our emotions. The truth is, when places, things, or people become emotionally draining, it means we actually were long aware of the decision we needed to make but just didn't make it. We continued charging forward with our life and as we did, the extra weight we carried started dragging behind us.

WORTH THE WEIGHT?

We all carry a little weight around, especially if you have to make important decisions all the time. The most unnecessary weight to carry around is the extra weight from an aimless relationship. This weight will come in the form of denial at first, then guilt, then frustration, then finally, resolution. The denial will keep you going back and forth in your mind about the situation — is this good, bad, right, wrong, for you or not for you. It causes a great deal of indecisiveness, which in turn hinders important effective decisions from being made, which then results in the guilt. You will feel like you should make one decision (cut things off) but then the consequences of that decision (being alone) will creep in. The fact that you solely will be responsible for said consequences will actually make it harder to proceed with the decision.

It is important to note that no matter what decisions you make, all decisions come with consequences and there is no need to let guilt in. Guilt keeps you weighed down with a feeling of being stuck and there is nothing you can do about your situation, which of course is not true. Nobody likes feeling as though they are stuck, and this feeling then inevitably produces frustration.

When we become mad at a situation but lack certain information or corrective actions, we turn that attention inward and this creates frustration.

Frustration can be powerful, both positively and negatively. It can also make you so blinded by your circumstance that you can't see past it. When you can't see past something that you feel is keeping you from moving forward, it can make you do things that become detrimental to your well-being. For example, imagine you're in your car on a narrow two-lane road and there is a big tractor trailer truck in front of you. Naturally, seeing past the truck is impossible. You don't know how long you will be behind the truck, whether it will turn first, or you will turn first, etc. I've been in this exact situation before and it was very frustrating and aggravating. If you allow the frustration to cause you to make the decision to drive past the truck, without the proper sight or surrounding information, you could be unknowingly driving into an accident waiting to happen. Life is like a highway with many exits and forks in the road. Making decisions will always be a requirement, but the ability to make proper decisions will always need to be developed. The point is this, although things can be frustrating, focusing on the frustration will not help you, it will only magnify the issue.

Let me clarify something here for you. When you break down what frustration actually is, it's simply *"expectation - patience."* Expectation minus patience equals frustration. The key to your frustrated situation is patience. You gain patience by gaining more information. The more information you have the more it will allow you to look at your situation correctly. Information helps you make better decisions. Remember when I said frustration is powerful? It's powerful in good ways too.

Once you get to the point where frustration causes you to gain new information again, it increases your patience, which then causes you to begin to value the version of yourself you felt was lost. Once that self-worth restoration happens, then your ability to make decisions that better your life leads you to resolutions. Although all of the ups and downs are good for learning, the place of resolve is the best place to be. Here, you can no longer be fooled because you've been fooled before. You can no longer be hurt because you've healed. You've arrived at the right place, and it's time to part ways with those things and people that have nothing to offer you. Like that narrow road, this is when you've accepted that you can't see past the truck, and have made the decision that at the first safe opportunity you get, you will remove yourself from the situation. The simple act of deciding takes your focus off the truck and puts it on the opportunities that arise to pass it. When resolution is guiding you, frustration no longer is.

RECAP CHAPTER 6:

In Business: An easy hire is a person who at the time of meeting them is unemployed, most times for periods of 6 months to a year, or even more, and seems very eager to land another job. It's never in your best interest to slow down productivity. Do your due diligence in your hiring process to make sure you avoid these candidates.

In Dating: The desperate-to-enter-a-relationship type are who you need to watch out for. Their main desire or objective is to just get into a relationship by any means. For them, a relationship represents a welcomed distraction and excuse to not pursue their personal goals. For you, it will cause frustration and stagnancy. Remember your Dating Preparation. Avoid these types or people or at least identify them early. They are not bad people; they just drag people, and you can do without the drag.

THE APPLICATION:

- Don't be so anxious that you compromise what you truly need.

- Avoid making decisions out of anxiousness.

- Don't carry around the unnecessary weight of an aimless relationship.

- Developing patience is how to overcome frustration.

CHAPTER 7

THE UNINTERESTED

(The Time Wasters)

IN BUSINESS

Imagine interviewing someone for Your Life, Inc. that clearly doesn't show high interest in the job, but you convince them to take it anyway. What you have just done is set yourself up for failure. How? It's simple. You've just hired someone on their terms rather than your company's terms, and as a result of this happening, you've now lost the ability to govern or manage your company as effectively as you desire. This is the beginning of a toxic foundation which is best prevented before it ever happens. If it has happened already, and you have identified it, let them go. There is never the perfect time to fire someone, it always will cost something. Would you rather it cost you now or later? It's better to have an open opportunity for the right person who wants the job, than the wrong one occupying space. Hiring decisions are always best when it's a mutual sentiment.

As a matter of fact, hiring decisions truly only work when it's mutual. If a candidate cannot see the vision, beauty, or benefit in what you have to offer, no matter how qualified or great they may be, they are doing you a favor by walking away or not filling a position. It's a favor to you because it should be evident that the role is really meant for someone else. Don't go chasing down those who want nothing to do with your company. Now, is it possible that the timing for that candidate you want is wrong and they're declining or aren't interested as a result? Sure! However, the needs of the business must come first. As the saying goes, "the show must go on." You must proceed forward with Your Life, Inc.'s decisions.

IN BUSINESS AND IN DATING

Funny enough, it was this exact thing that I experienced in both business and dating that became the catalyst for this book. I once dated a girl, whom I was really into, for close to two years. It seemed only natural, then, to start talking about the next level for us. However, I didn't start out being intentional. I wasn't looking for a wife and I didn't start out with a reasonable time frame in which things should progress. Back then, I was a mere shell of the man I am today, and while I can honestly say I am thankful for all my previous experiences, I believe too many relationships start out this way.

Because certain key foundational things are not put in place, they start with the "let's-have-fun" approach and later face an uphill battle when they try to shift into something serious. In my case, while dating this girl and running my business, I began to see similar behavioral traits between her and one of my employees. My approach to each of them, however, was very different. The main difference was that for me as a businessman, business decisions are far easier to make because they're often void of emotion. If I saw an employee that was slacking or displaying low interest in the job, my first instinct was to cut them off. Yet, like most people, that same behavior expressed in a relationship would often receive second chance after second chance after seventh chance. Why is that? It's because in this area our emotions are fully involved in our decision-making.

In business, the saying, "It's nothing personal, just business," has become the North star for progression and has been the status quo for decades. Get this; did you know the phrase was actually coined by Otto Biederman, an accountant and advisor for an American gangster named Dutch Schultz? I can understand why he said it too. Biederman, by profession, dealt with numbers, and numbers are absolutes. For him, I'm sure it was far easier to deal with things that were absolutes versus all the other morally gray areas, which included murder, bootlegging, or racketeering. Everything does have an origin I suppose, but nonetheless, this statement alone has caused a lot of tough, cut-throat and innovative decisions to be made that helped move the world forward. It's meant to help us override the often-complicated process that emotions create for us. After all, emotions are just feelings. This is not to discredit our feelings; they do have a purpose. However, with the way our feelings can change daily and instantaneously, we shouldn't rely heavily on them. We need to make sure the disconnect and detach button works for our personal decisions also, not just business ones.

When my girlfriend said to me, "I don't know if I want to be in this relationship anymore," I fought with everything in me to prove that she should. We stayed together (off and on) for almost another year after that point before it abruptly ended. Yet, had my employee said blatantly to me, "I don't know if I want to work here anymore," the decision to help them exit, without malice, would be a no-brainer for me. This is an example of two people practically saying the exact same thing, and yet, because of the emotional connection to one—which alone may not be the greatest foundation—is enough to keep someone from valuing themselves and results in wasting time. This is why you should not only desire to stay away from the Uninterested (time-wasters), but you ought to know exactly how to identify them. Keep reading. I'm going to show you how—and I truly hope you're not one of them.

UNREALISTIC EXPECTATIONS

They say true love is unconditional. While I don't feel this statement is truly embodied to the fullest, I agree with its intention, which is to love in such a way that condition doesn't dictate the decision one has made to love. If you truly love someone, there shouldn't be anything that can make your love for them become less. Is this really true though? When most people say those three amazing words, "I love you," they are not unconditional. In fact, when people say these amazing words to others, most of the time they don't really know what they are saying, or even why they are saying it.

The very first person you and I learned those words from set the foundation of what it means for us. When we were babies and learning how to do just about everything, we constantly heard "I love you, I love you." Some will say it's because our parents really meant it, but I will say it's because we were cute could-barely-do-anything-for- ourselves little people that became sponges for their affection. When we finally learned how to say it back, all those months of our parents investing their time and affection into us finally seemed worth it. They could get a return on that emotional investment and I can bet it felt good. Even as babies, we could see that it made them feel good when we said it to them. So, what did we do? We continued to say it to make them feel good. On a bad day, we made them feel good. When they got mad at us, we made them feel good. When they got us gifts, we made them feel good. And now, subtly, over time "I love you" becomes the currency we exchange in order to feel good and make others feel good. I'm not saying this is wrong, I'm just letting you know "love" as we know it isn't unconditional. It's very much conditional and has been that way our whole life. The truth is, to love one another is a law (read your Bible) which should never change. To be in love or to be loved, however, is a feeling, and feelings change all the time. Failure to understand this can create some unrealistic expectations.

Are you currently with someone who has told you, "When you {insert act or deed here} then I will {do this or that}?" The girl I mentioned earlier that I was dating for two years told me, "We could get married if you buy me a house first." You may be thinking that's not too unrealistic of an expectation. It all depends; these things are all relative. To some folks living in the Southern states or even the Midwest of the United States it may not be unrealistic. I was born and raised in North Carolina so I know this. A $300,000 home where I'm from might get you 5 beds, 5 baths, and 5900 square feet. However, in Los Angeles, California, where I live, those metrics would be nonexistent, and therefore such expectations are a bit unrealistic. Not impossible, just unrealistic. If I recall correctly, at the time she was living with her mom in an apartment. I hope you get what I'm saying. When you experience what sounds like unrealistic expectations, it usually means there's a very low interest in having a future with you. In other words, it's a big waste of time! The sooner you can identify the time wasters, the better.

IN BUSINESS

The same is true for Your Life, Inc. Not everyone who has agreed to take the job agrees with your vision and the vision you have for them. It's similar to the millennial behavior that you always see or hear about. I'm separating millennial behavior from Millennials because, not only are they two different things, but up until the point of their dominance, things in the world seemingly were very traditional. Millennials have changed the landscape of business and marriage as we know it, especially when it comes to employment tenure and the age of settling down in relationships.

When most think of the term Millennials, they believe it's describing the young in age or a stage in life, but that's not the case. We all belong to a particular generational class based on a year of birth range, namely Baby Boomers, Generation X, Generation Y, Generation Z and the new kids on the block, Generation Alpha—which sounds pretty cool. Although the date range seems to change from source to source, you will always be a part of the generation you started with. Now, with this general understanding about the generational classifications, we're going to look at the popular millennial behavior because, as I stated, they have changed the landscape of business and marriage.

For starters, millennials are said to not be as engaged as the traditional employee. According to Gallup research studies on millennials in 2018, they are the least engaged generation; only 20 percent are engaged, while 55 percent are not engaged, leaving 16 percent actively disengaged. Some may like the pay when they start but feel deserving of a raise after only a short time. For you, as the boss, a raise may not be feasible until some time further out, but to them, because they want it now, it may be worth it to start looking elsewhere. It's generally said of Millennials that they don't believe in long-term occupational commitment, unlike their parents the Baby Boomers, who were mostly married in their late teens and early twenties. Baby Boomers were also known to work the same job for close to 30 years or more. Millennials change jobs more often than others in the workforce who came before them. Whether it's because they don't like the benefits package or think promotions aren't happening fast enough, statistics show that roughly 21 percent reported switching jobs within the last year and 60 percent are open to different opportunities.

This means that right now, as we speak, though they may look busy at work, some are getting paid while using their laptops to look for other jobs. In fact, their turnover costs the U.S. economy an estimated $30.5 billion annually. You have to make sure you know exactly who you are staffing your company with and why. Not everyone on your team is going to give 100 percent, and not everyone has your best interest in mind. Not everyone is more concerned about your bottom line than their own bottom. To put it plainly, the unrealistic, millennial behavior depicts the "uninterested." Anyone who is not interested in a thing will drag their feet on tasks you give them and have you drained of more energy than you were expected to give.

This doesn't mean they're bad. They just think differently, and this book wasn't written to judge a person's character. We are here to merely evaluate how to make decisions that help us spend time on things that are benefiting our interests and less time on things that don't. Moreover, some business models like the fast-food industry are built with high expected turnover rates. Many of us as teenagers shared the same mindset as what is now considered millennial behavior, and most likely worked a job flipping burgers or something similar. I shared that my first enjoyable job was at Blockbuster Video, but my actual first job as an employee was with a small company called McDonalds. I loved having a job, along with their apple pies, but it wasn't long after I got it that I was looking for a better job and another opportunity. This is why I believe this behavior has existed long before the generational name was created and marketed as "Millennial" exclusively. If you are a traditional person, with traditional values and goals for your company, then your business model will need to include loyal personnel, along with the ability to adapt with the times.

in dating

As an intentional, high-functioning person, when you meet someone you're interested in, you should be able to ask the right questions and discern if they are worth your time from the very beginning. It doesn't matter how attractive a person is, be aware that you don't get time back. A person's behavior will tell you everything you need to know, therefore don't entertain the uninterested for longer than you have to (If you're already in a relationship with the uninterested, find the courage to let them go). When people fade out of your life, they are doing you a huge favor. Never try to talk someone into staying with you. It doesn't matter how wonderful they are or how attracted you are to them, you can't make someone call, care or love you that doesn't want to. It doesn't mean the person who left was a bad person, it just means their story in the chapter of your book is over. Say goodbye, there is a reason and purpose behind everything. There is never a perfect time to break up with someone. If you notice that there hasn't been any progression in your relationship for quite some time, nor is there a plan of action on the table, the best time is always now—especially before too much emotional fog sets in and clogs your clarity. Clear your emotional fog by seeing things as they are, not what you hope they become. Take a moment, and read that statement again. In any other area of life, it's okay to have that sort of faith, but when it comes to people who have their own free will, it's highly unwise. Take note when people show you how much they value you and your time. You should always be the clear choice, never the option. You should be with someone who wants to invest in your life and motivates you to become your best version. They should want to see you win and support your vision. We have to develop a level of maturity that allows us to see when growth is no longer happening and when to let someone or something go. If the people you date aren't growing, or if you're not growing as a result of being with them, then it's time to let go of the time wasters.

RECAP CHAPTER 7:

In Business: There is never the perfect time to fire someone, it will always cost something. The question is always, what are you willing to pay for it? A candidate should see the value of your company. Don't hire someone you have to convince to value your company. If you do, you're setting yourself up for failure. Why? Because you will have accepted them on their terms and lose the ability to govern or manage your company as effectively as you desire. This is the beginning of a toxic foundation which is best prevented before it ever happens.

In Dating: There is never a perfect time to break up with someone, it will always cost you something. The question is always, what are you willing to pay for it? Don't entertain the uninterested for longer than you have to. As an intentional, high-functioning person, when you meet someone you're interested in, you should be able to ask the right questions and discern if they are worth your time from the very beginning.

THE APPLICATION:

- If you're always the option and never the clear choice, you should leave before you get left behind.

- Separate from those who don't value you and your time, find the right people who will. Never try to oversell your dream or your personal value.

- Know that love does have conditions, but they shouldn't be unrealistic.

- Understand a person sharing their unrealistic expectations is sharing their low interest in having a future with you.

- Remember, the best relationships start with mutual decisions.

- Understand there will always be a cost for what you want, either now or later.

CHAPTER 8

THE TOP RECRUITS

(The Ones Everybody Wants)

IN BUSINESS

In every walk of life, whether business, sports, politics or otherwise, there have always been certain types of people that, for good reason, stood out from the rest. This will most likely never change, because these people only know how to focus on one thing—winning. And many times, winning at all costs. The people that we're talking about here are known as Top Recruits. Like anyone, Top recruits have their upside and downside, and we're going to examine both.

On the upside, their reputation exhibits great self-confidence and independence. They are assertive and set the bar exceptionally high in their respective fields. They know their self-worth and how to put their value on display. They also understand power dynamics and how to influence people. With these traits, they garner attention from everyone, especially unassertive individuals. Decision makers, regardless of industry, recognize these strong, talented individuals and seek to reward or retain them by any means necessary. The unassertive people who passively accept the conditions around them, instead of becoming inspired, usually incite different emotions which impact their productivity in a negative way. In other words, they allow their personal shortcomings and insecurities to dominate their thoughts and thus reduce their own potential and output. This dilemma by default can create an even higher value for those who are strongly talented. Top recruits are usually good people and their value is priceless.

On the downside, the one issue you can run into with the majority of them is they've only ever been told how great they are and have believed it. You might ask, what's the problem with that? Shouldn't we believe in ourselves? Yes, we absolutely should. However, we ought to have a healthy understanding of our strengths as well as our weaknesses in order to know what balance looks like. If all we hear is how great we are and never what we need to work on to get better, it produces a false sense of reality within us as well as a lack of humility. Whenever a healthy balance is lacking it tends to produce confidence's annoying cousin, arrogance. Arrogance is an attitude or display of superiority or self-importance. While it is okay to have confidence in yourself, if you get to the point where you think the sun rises and sets only for you, then you passed confidence about three exits back.

Top recruits can do absolute wonders for Your Life, Inc. because they're results-driven. Unfortunately, they may not plan to stay long enough for you to see results happen. Why? Because they know they are highly sought after. The world and the people they encounter tend to bend the rules for them a little bit. Actually, a lot. Standards and deadlines are often changed because they're regularly treated as the exception to the rule. Not to mention the reality that the majority of people in society aren't living to their fullest potential and being their true selves. Therefore, when a Top Recruit steps on the scene, the self-assurance they carry automatically produces self-reflection and self-evaluation in others, often causing them to see their flaws and inefficiencies. In other words, they're able to blind people with their assuredness.

In hiring situations, these people are seen as coming in at the right time, in the best attire, with the best resumes, from the right schools, and with all the right skill sets. Once a company identifies this candidate, they immediately get ahead of themselves and believe their company will be stronger and better. With top recruits, no company (even Your Life, Inc.) can or should expect to retain them for long. Remember how I said that they're results-driven and focused on winning? That mentality unfortunately causes them to see the need to keep their options open at all times. The main question that replays in their mind, which becomes their filtering process is, "What can you offer me?" Or more specifically, "What can the next company offer me that this one can't?"

Let me give you an example. Imagine that Company A is currently in a one-story building with fewer than 10 parking spaces and with fewer than 10 employees working in their cubicles. All employees get a ten-minute grace period to arrive to work so they're not rushing in the morning and made to feel bad for being late. There is a break room for the employees located in the back corner of the facility, equipped with a mini fridge, a coffee maker, a few tables and chairs. They're allowed a lunch break of 30 minutes and given two 15-minute rest breaks. They have every major holiday off, with the exception of maybe two, Labor Day and Memorial Day, and most have to report back to work the following day. Additionally, they have the occasional get together for holiday parties and maybe receive a bonus or two. This sounds like a good company that cares about its employees, right? To an Easy Hire perhaps, but in the majority of cases, a Top Recruit is looking for more, for a better deal. They may take one or two of your interviews and even tour your company. Then right when they have you believing that landing them is a possibility, they boldly let you know they have other interviews or offers they want to entertain. You might even get hit with, "I'll let you know sometime next week." Company A may have offered them the very best it had to offer, but Company B across town with its three-story building, over 100 parking spots, 100 employees all with security keycards and company credit cards, 401K plans, big individual offices to enjoy 1-hour naps, employee cafeteria to enjoy 1-hour lunches, flexibility of schedule, sick days, all holidays off and paid, with hefty annual bonuses, frankly could offer more.

Years ago, I needed to fill one of the more vital roles in my company. I interviewed several people but came across this one candidate with an amazing resume. He had the experience I was looking for and the advanced skill set that would've made him a top recruit in our industry. I recognized the opportunity mid interview and knew the guy most definitely had the job as long as the interview ended well, which it did. I was ready to offer him the job and hire him on the spot, something I'd never done at the time. I asked for his availability and when he would be able to start. He then told me he would have to get back to me because he had two other interviews with two other companies and he didn't want to do anything with scheduling too prematurely. Though I respected the candor, I knew he wouldn't have said that had he liked the facility and all we had to offer him. He was saying to me in a very professional manner, "If I can't get more or I don't like them better then I will give you a call." I didn't see anything wrong with that sentiment at the time because I was a young business owner. I also had not yet made the correlation upon which this chapter is founded. Moreover, some companies have a habit of not wanting to appear desperate or anxious even if they like you for the job, so they wait to call you in two weeks to let you know the job is yours. This of course is a dated practice, but depending on supply and demand it is still used. The first week after the interview, I remember my excitement was at a high thinking the open position was going to be filled by this amazingly qualified person. I felt a great weight lifting off my shoulders. By the second week, I contacted the candidate only to learn he had accepted another job offer the week before. I was a bit bummed out but couldn't stay that way because the show must go on. The moral of this story is, when someone doesn't see the value of your company as you would like them to, move on because the show goes on.

Although it is tempting to fight for these types, you shouldn't. It is important to accept when you've done all that you can so you know not to waste your time with these candidates. The truth is, although Company B clearly had more to offer, a Top Recruit unfortunately will never be satisfied. They soon will need to entertain Company C, D, E, F, G, H, I, J, and so on. It's a cycle that keeps on repeating itself. Eventually, they will find a place to land and get settled, which will usually come after they've experienced the right deal and a great deal of time passes.

in dating

Expectedly, there are also Top Recruits in dating. Have you ever met someone very attractive who always dresses well, is well groomed, smells good and has great things going for them professionally? When you encounter these types of people, they dull your receptors a bit and engulf you in their aura. Time and rules seem to blur a little bit, as they both seem to have less importance for a moment. Just talking to them excites you, brings a surge of energy and makes you feel better. Being seen with them gives you a sense of accomplishment and automatically gains you more popularity. Or have you ever felt like every time you were interested in someone, that everybody else was too? All these, my friend, are just a few indicators that you have met someone of high value in dating, known as a Top Recruit. As I mentioned earlier, they aren't bad, they are simply products of their environments, just as we all are. The conditions around us reinforce the ways we think. Their way of thinking is mainly a result of only receiving countless positive reinforcements regarding their physical or other attributes over the course of their life. And I get it. If you tell a good-looking person that they look great all the time without highlighting their non-physical attributes the same way, it can make a person only focus on or use those attributes to their benefit. I'm not saying they're not smart, because the majority of them are super smart. However, what they are or what they learn to be is an opportunist.

An opportunist is a person who exploits circumstances to gain immediate advantage rather than being guided by consistent principles or plans. It doesn't matter whether they entertain you or for how long, eventually they are going to be looking for more. You can only offer a person what you have available to give. So please understand, the issue is not you. Seriously, it's not. They know this too. They know that if they or the current opportunity begin to feel underwhelming, they're going to seek other opportunities elsewhere in order to feel their value and worth again. As weird as this may sound, it's a cycle that many of them stay in for quite a while...a long while. It's not an infinite time loop, but it continues until they decide to finally settle down with the right person. Dating them is not for the faint of heart, but I believe those reading this book know this already. It's tempting to make excuses for them and say they're just distracted, but don't do that to yourself. Read the signs.

Top recruits are the people others want. They know it and they want to be wanted. What if you're dating one of them already? This is usually the equation that eventually leads to the end of the relationship: on one hand you see a value because you also can benefit from the association, but on the other hand they only see value where it benefits them. I'm not saying this is right, it's just life. Some people think "the grass is greener" elsewhere and that becomes their motivation to keep going after certain things.

Unfortunately, it's usually not until you're standing on said grass that you realize it's only greener because you decided it was. That same realization could've come years prior, but with the way life is set up, these types like to control their narratives. They must see what else is out there and what can be offered to them.

I repeat, Top Recruits aren't bad people, they're just people in high demand. Though they may entertain you for a bit, they genuinely don't want their time wasted or to waste anyone else's time. Their thinking is, the sooner they can get out of the way the sooner the right person for you will come. I remember years ago in my mid-twenties, way before I ever met my wife, I had a situation-ship with a young lady. She was very adamant that she wanted me and no one else in her life as her man. I, on the other hand, was not ready for that kind of commitment. I desired to move from North Carolina to California and chase my dreams, which I did, and though she wanted to follow me, she had a different set of responsibilities than I did. She had gotten married young but got divorced, and had two beautiful kids from that relationship. I thought she was attractive, bright and funny, but still wasn't ready for such a big commitment. At that time, you could've called me a time-waster. As time passed and we kept in touch, she told me that there was a guy who was madly in love with her but she didn't want to commit to him. Anytime I came into town and gave her a call, she was ready to drop everything to arrange for us to be together, babysitter and all. We would hang out and have fun, but it only made her want me more. Frankly, I was benefiting from her physical offerings but didn't want to invest emotionally. Although I was upfront with her about all of these things, it didn't stop her from trying to convince me otherwise. Months went by and there she was, still responding to me but keeping the other guy around as a plan b. She informed me that he had brought an engagement ring and was serious about moving forward with her but she still didn't want to. Though it took me some time to realize I was the problem, once I knew it, I removed myself from her situation entirely. After a little more time had passed, I later learned she and the guy finally got married. Now they have a beautiful family. While in that situation I still wanted to see what life or the world had to offer me and didn't see how her company could compete with it. I'm not telling this story for you to hate me, because we all grow; I'm telling you this because although it is just one example of many, that type of mindset is held by millions of people without the same action to follow. When I saw the problem was me, I changed the situation. Indeed, it was a selfless thing to do, but it was also an easy one. Why? Because I was in demand. It was never personal, but that's how it can feel in relationships. If more people understand this, then I believe we can curb the bad decisions made by broken hearts and help millions of people get on with their lives. Also, though this will be featured in the later *Disclaimer* chapter, I want to highlight that we all can easily be this type of person to someone else. Every candidate you read about could be or has been you at some point. The great thing is all candidates have the ability to change, much of which naturally happens when time and maturity are added to the equation.

Reflect for a moment. Do you currently have anyone in your life with these kinds of habits or patterns? If so, do yourself a favor and let them go. If your emotions are tying you to this person but their actions are not favorable towards you, don't support them; let them go. I'm saying this in love because if you don't let them go now while you have the strength, eventually they will let you go and cost you some unnecessary pain later. Open your eyes and really try to identify these people when they cross your path. There is definitely something to be gained from the encounter, but don't let the gain turn to pain. The adage, "no pain, no gain," is true, but so is, "fool me once, shame on you; fool me twice, shame on me." I'd like to add my own, and maybe we can make this into a thing, "no shame, no pain, just gain."

RECAP CHAPTER 8:

In Business: Top recruits only know how to focus on winning at all costs. On the upside, their reputation exhibits great self-confidence and independence. On the downside, they have believed in their own hype so much to the point that it costs others. They are also capable of being arrogant. Top recruits can do absolute wonders for Your Life, Inc. because they're results driven. Unfortunately, they may not plan to stay long enough for you to see results happen. It is important to accept when you've done all that you can so you know not to waste your time with these candidates.

In Dating: Have you ever met someone very attractive who always dresses well, is well groomed, smells good and has great things going for them professionally? This is considered a Top recruit. Top recruits are the people others want. They know it and they want to be wanted. Some people think "the grass is greener" elsewhere and that's their motivation to keep going after certain things. Top recruits aren't bad people, they're just people in high demand. Though they may entertain you for a bit, they genuinely don't want their time wasted or to waste anyone else's time. Their thinking is the sooner they can get out of the way, the sooner the right candidate for you will come.

THE APPLICATION:

- Learn from Top Recruits, don't get burned by them.
- High value is determined by what qualities you offer.
- You can only offer your best, nothing more.
- Know that it's good to be confident, but also learn humility.
- When someone shows you who they are, believe them, don't try to change them.

CHAPTER 9

GAME CHANGERS – Part 1

(God's Gift To Someone)

Game changer – a newly introduced element or factor that changes an existing situation or activity in a significant way.

IN BUSINESS

This next portion of information was to be contained in one chapter but I decided to expound it in two parts. Trust me, it will be worth your time. What we are about to discuss is extremely important. Having a plan for how you want Your Life, Inc. to operate is essential because it gives you the necessary structural and governing guidelines to determine what method your company should use to handle the unforeseeable obstacles in its future. As CEO, the responsibility of steering the ship through troubled or unpredictable waters usually falls on you. You may have a team, but you're the captain. This is just one of the many reasons why this role is so special and vital to a company's success, part of which begins when the company can determine how and who it hires. While most companies are well-meaning, their lack of thoroughness at the onset of interviewing candidates only results in creating busy work for themselves that leads to nothing. The focus should always be on acquiring the best quality of candidates, not the highest quantity. If this is executed poorly, it can become costly to refill positions because, inevitably, high turnover will be imminent.

High turnover can often be more of a distraction than an opportunity, and when we are distracted, we miss things. Especially the things right under our nose. Believe it or not, the most special people and opportunities we are to encounter in this life are usually right in front of us. I truly believe most companies desire to hire the right people, but practicably fail to do so. The lack of vision or presence of too many distractions causes many companies to fail in hiring that one person who not only understands the current state of the company and where it can go, but also wants to greatly contribute to it getting there. This unique individual is called a Game Changer.

By definition, a game changer is a newly introduced element or factor that changes an existing situation or activity in a significant way. Game changers are innovators. These are people who, at first, may appear very unassuming, but are actually the very people who are meant to shift Your Life, Inc. for the foreseeable future. They have been known to seek you out before there is even a job available, and as a result they often get overlooked due to their timing. It's not their timing that is bad, however, it's yours. Your job as the boss is to know exactly what you are looking for, create opportunities, and then choose wisely. If you do this, it should be hard for you to miss them.

Game changers are usually the very qualified yet most humble people who are quietly waiting for the right moment to present itself. When they come along, you don't have to put in much work to convince them of your vision. Not only can they see it very clearly, they can also see what the missing pieces are. In fact, their job is to add that missing piece and make Your Life, Inc. more successful. That is, if you are open and willing to allow them to; many times, game changers show up when you're not ready for them. They show up when you're in need of a change and for something new, but you have not realized it yet. Because your destiny knows this, however, they are released to you. Have you ever heard of the saying, "when the student is ready the teacher will appear?" It's a similar thing that happens. When Your Life, Inc. is ready, the game changers will appear.

Here's a small tip regarding game changers: One way you will recognize them is by the amount of resistance you will want to give them at first. The resistance won't be because they're saying all the wrong things, but because the things they say will challenge everything you know, causing you to look at things differently for the first time in a long time. Game changers are there to tell you not only what you are doing wrong, but also how to improve on what you are doing. They will point out things that you haven't thought of yet or been open to, and since these are not your ideas, that intrusion-of-privacy feeling will tend to cause your guard to instantly go up. However, if you can choose to ignore that feeling and take a chance with them, it will only be a matter of time before you see the benefits of what was said, and consequently, begin to give more value to the person who said it. It's important to recognize who your superstars are. If you are wise in running your company, anything that creates value for you should be too valuable to lose or turn away.

STARS GENERATE BUCKS

One game changer I'd like to talk about, who not only was resisted at first, but later created such a high value for themself that things came back around, is Howard Schultz. He is the man responsible for the Starbucks chain as we know it today. Howard Schultz's first job after college was selling office equipment door-to-door. Even though he would make up to fifty cold calls each day, he enjoyed talking to people and was pretty good at sales. He eventually worked for a European company that made housewares, and one of his customers was a small coffee company in Seattle, Washington named Starbucks. In 1982, he went to visit the founders, and within a year, he was heading up marketing for Starbucks and had moved to Seattle with his wife. The following year, he was on a business trip to Italy when he walked into an Italian café and tasted his very first espresso. The beverage captivated him, the barista who prepared it impressed him, and the atmosphere of the café engulfed him. At the time, Starbucks stores only sold whole bean coffee and had no seating. Schultz had a vision of creating specialty coffee stores that integrated the romance of espresso and provided a place for community. The founders of

Starbucks however, Jerry Baldwin and Gordon Bowker, were not interested in his idea.

Schultz left Starbucks in 1985 to open a store of his own. He visited over 500 espresso bars in Milan, and, with him assuming most of the risk associated, he set out to introduce espresso to the American market. He needed $400,000 to start his business, and Starbucks invested $150,000 in the new venture, with Baldwin receiving a place on its board and Bowker offering unofficial assistance. Another $100,000 came from a local doctor. Of the 242 investors Schultz approached, 217 rejected his idea. By 1986, he had raised the money he needed to open his first store, II Giornale, named after the Milanese newspaper. The store offered ice cream in addition to coffee, had little seating, and played opera music in the background. Two years later, the original Starbucks management team decided to focus on Peet's Coffee & Tea and sold its Starbucks retail unit to Schultz and II Giornale for $3.8 million.

Schultz rebranded Il Giornale with the Starbucks name, and expanded its reach across the United States. The rest we know is grande, or should I say, venti!

"I never set out to build a global business. I set out to build the kind of company that my father never had a chance to work for—one that treats all people with dignity." –Howard Schultz

Howard Schultz, a lot like the late Steve Jobs, before becoming a great CEO, was the ultimate Game Changer. If these men were less intentional about the things they wanted to achieve, then we wouldn't know their companies as we know them today. What we see in both of them is the ability to add different and fresh ideas to an existing thing in order for it to transform into something greater.

Let's evaluate Your Life, Inc. for a moment. Do you currently have anyone around you or within your company that is like this? Is there anyone who is constantly showing interest and asking about your future plans? Are they sharing their solutions and bright ideas with you, whether solicited or not? Do they honor your time and show respect to you? Do they treat you as a high value person? Are you resisting them the same way Starbucks and Apple did? Stop and think about these questions. Many times, most people have their Game Changer right in front of them but fail to see it.

in dating

Your Game Changer is a person who might have strong or bright ideas on how you can achieve future personal goals. They see a quality in you that maybe even you don't see. They will also start involving themselves in your goals and use words around you like "we", "us", and "our". For example, you might say, "I need to get in shape," and they may follow up with something like, "I've been meaning to get in shape also; we can work out whenever you want." Or you might say something like, "I need new clothes," and they follow up with something like, "We can go shopping together, I think I know what'll look good on you." Did you catch that? Do you see the inclusion? Do you see the way they keep integrating themselves into your plans? This person wants to help and be an aid to you. This person is God's gift to you.

When you live past a certain point, you realize that attention or popularity fades to a degree. People in their 20s may feel invincible or like they're on top of the world, or even that the world owes them something. In your 30s or 40s however, you begin to see that life works a little differently. The world isn't checking for you like that anymore, and neither are people.

134

They have their own lives, problems, bills, worries, and goals to distract them. At this age, you start to realize that thinking you have time to waste is an illusion. I know people often say YOLO (you only live once), which is true, but they use it as a license to live recklessly. Indeed, your youth should be lived boldly, but your focus should always be on how you can set up your future in the best possible way. I'm not saying turn into some gold digger, but rather be a goal digger. Listen, young ladies, it would be wise to use your 20s and your beauty to your advantage in finding your life partner, not just simply living it up. I know girls just want to have fun or have their hot girl summers, but at what cost? Before you know it, you'll find yourself on a girl's trip, single, in your late 30s, reflecting on life and wondering what opportunities you missed. I personally believe around the cusp of age 35, single women especially, begin to choose between relationship and career. In other words, they turn their careers into their relationships. Don't wait until it's too late to act; turn things around while you have time. The same goes for the young gentleman. Having a goal is good, but having a plan to obtain that goal is better. As men, our main concern, especially when we are young, is having enough money. The truth is, if that is already your mindset in your 20s, and you make certain decisions based on that, then you'll never have enough in your 30s, 40s, or 50s. I'm not saying you won't find success; I know you will. I'm saying, you'll never have enough if your goal is solely to have it. So, what should you do? As men, it's crucial that we are as grounded as possible. This means, have real tangible plans and make real tangible goals. Additionally, set reasonable milestones in your life and achieve them step by step. Instead of saying, in ten years you're going to XYZ, set a goal 2-3 years out as well so that you can better gauge your progress toward your long-term goals. Why? That way you won't get too distracted by the big picture or outcome and miss the opportunities sent to help you get there. You should also use what you've been given—your youthful looks, intelligence, time, energy and determination for success—to find someone to build your future with. All those things you want, you can and will have, with the right relationship.

A majority of people think they need to have certain things in order before they can get in the right relationship. Even though they say they don't want to settle, that same majority, unfortunately, find themselves hoping and praying their time or opportunity for love hasn't passed them by. The good news is, it hasn't! For starters, it is important that you keep in mind that you're not settling; you're simply settling down, which is the goal. Settling down takes a different type of maturity that most think they are ready for, but in reality, are not. The main requirement is for you to be open minded. Your game changer is probably close by, so stop and look around. Are you willing to accept them? Are you keeping a watchful eye and an open mind that will enable you to recognize potential when you see it versus how you expect it to be? Are you being practical— maintaining sober and logical thinking towards your rational goals in order to reach them? All these are key components when it comes to meeting your game changer.

Let's look at 3 main ways your game changer can be identified. Number one is by their Commitment. They faithfully check-in.

They're drawn to you and acknowledge your goals. Secondly is Inclusion. They want to help you reach your goals so badly they include themselves in your plans. Thirdly is Execution. They look for ways to get the things you need done. Whenever you see these 3 characteristics in a person, anchor down, because they may just be your game changer. Moreover, if some of these sound or look familiar to you, it's probably because they are. If you are currently over the age of 35, single, and honest with yourself, you may recall that you've encountered people with these or very similar attributes at one point in your life but you took them for granted. In other words, you've just been too picky. You might've even said something like, "they're too..." this or that—nice, short, annoying, goofy, loud, etc. If any of these rings a bell, and if you ever said this in the past, it was because you were probably the most valued in the situation at the time. Notice I said 'most valued' and not 'valuable.' This is because you were simply the most valued of the two of you. Dare I say, maybe even a Top Recruit at one point. It's not your fault, you couldn't see who they were at the time. However, things change—they always do and they always will. Therefore, it's important that you understand why it's not your fault that you couldn't see them for who they were.

WHY IT'S NOT YOUR FAULT

For starters, I'm a firm believer that we're all products of our environment. If this is true, then that means every thought, like or dislike, quirk and characteristic we have comes from our environment. Essentially, we've been influenced all our lives both knowingly and unknowingly. Since you've been born you've been learning, even though there was a time you didn't always know what was happening. Everything you know, you adopted from somewhere. This is how powerful our environment is, and once we know how it influences us, then we can understand how to use it to our advantage, especially for single people. Single people listen up. I'm about to simplify your life with one statement, and even if you close the book right after, you will have enough information to improve your life dramatically. Ready? Here it goes: <u>The majority of the time your husband or wife is right in front of you, in the same environment.</u> Boom! I said it, and it's true. They're literally hiding in plain sight at your job, in your church, in your neighborhood or in your circle of friends. How is it that you don't see them? First off, we have to dispel a couple of things. One, fantasy Hollywood movies, especially Disney, have lied to you; and two, there is no soul mate for you, not in the way you think. Now that I have your attention, let's go a bit deeper.

When we were little children, our imaginations were big. As kids, movies made it easy for us to believe anything. I remember one time after I found a bird's feather on the ground, my uncle happened to walk by and said, "if you find another one, you'll be able to fly." I don't know if he was making a Dumbo joke due to my big ears at the time or not (of course he was) but I believed him. I remember walking outside my grandmother's house searching and searching for this second feather. I found one. It was bigger than the first one I'd found, but my uncle didn't say it had to be the same size. With both feathers in hand, I walk up the steps of my grandmother's high porch, stood right on the very edge, then with a single thrust of my legs, I closed my eyes as I took a big leap in the air, flapping my arms furiously, expecting to at least clip the top of the tree she had in the center of her yard, all for just moments later to feel my feet crash land on the ground. Needless to say, I quickly gave it another try but was heartbroken when the results didn't change. Why was I heartbroken? Was it because my uncle lied to me or because I really wanted to fly? No. It was because I believed in movies and fairy tales.

As responsible adults, we make plans. I stated earlier that having plans for how you want things in your life to operate is great. Plans, however, require flexibility. There is a passage in Proverbs that says, "We can make our plans, but the Lord determines our steps." For most of us, the plans we made started when we were children. Anything is possible in the mind of a child. This is actually the trait that makes kids so special. But what happens when well-meaning intentions put false narratives in the mind of a child? Well, they essentially will believe they can fly with a feather, just to become upset when they realize they can't. In other words, something can be made true in our minds for decades long until the reality of the matter arrives to correct it, usually at a cost. For a vast majority, getting married or being married is one of the first things we're made to believe in as little girls and boys. This makes sense, especially if you had both dad and mom in the same house growing up. However, while a loving, two-parent image can go a long way, if you didn't have this to look at, you had something else that was just as powerful, namely Disney movies and Hollywood make-believe. Now, I'm not making this an essay against Disney, I have no beef with them. Unfortunately, as adults, we regularly learn in very sobering ways that our Prince Charmings don't ride on horses neither do our Princesses live in castles with servants, nor do they need saving. Instead, they might currently have a roommate or a one-bedroom apartment, and they might even be driving a Honda, if they have a car at all. It's important that reality sets in and we acknowledge that what we were made to believe as children has played a major part in our expectations. The two most common expectations of life are of perfection and having all the time we want.

Typically, when we think we know exactly what we want in a partner, we develop what is referred to as 'types'. Types are simply people we place in a certain category. We start dating particular types because we're attracted to them and they fit our image of perfection. Oftentimes we always pay the price and learn that the relationships with our types all end in similar ways, disappointment. When this happens, we panic because that image we've held onto since childhood begins to shatter, and we start to see life is a little more complicated than we thought. However, there is one saving grace. You can still watch your favorite romantic comedy or movie that tells you, "It's okay and to keep hope alive, and that your perfect person is still out there." So, you believe again, think you have more time, and become even more selective, or better known as super-picky.

It's easy to believe you have all this time when you're young or just believe that you do. And it's because of these expectations we purposely miss the opportunities to connect with available people. This type of thinking actually is only decreasing your chances of finding the right partner. With you now being so selective, it's easy to believe that at the appointed time you will meet the one you've always been waiting for, your soul mate. It's time to feel your feet crash and land on the ground. There is no soul mate, at least not the way you think.

I found this definition of soul mate that I wanted to share. It is by far the most believed definition and expectation when you think of a soul mate. "A soul mate is a person with whom you have an immediate connection the moment you meet—a connection so strong that you are drawn to them in a way you have never experienced before. As this connection develops over time, you experience a love so deep, strong and complex, that you begin to doubt that you have ever truly loved anyone prior. Your soul mate understands and connects with you in every way and on every level, which brings a sense of peace, calmness and happiness when you are around them." That's deep. Couldn't you fall in love just reading those words? That definition right there is the reason why people are still single and why Hollywood continues to make billions of dollars. Well, not billions of dollars on rom-coms, but I digress. I'm not saying it's impossible to have these experiences with someone, as I'm sure some people have, and maybe a few have been able to turn them into something lasting. To be frank, if you're reading this book, then you know that the definition you just read is possibly something you've not only felt before, but may have caused you to justify many actions and ultimately lead to what is called a toxic relationship. Trust me, I've had a few. The main problem with this definition is it primarily transforms a soul mate into nothing more than feelings; a person becomes some deep, strong, and passionate connection. The thing about feelings, however, is that they change.

Another definition, that I actually like, says, "a soul mate is a person ideally suited to another as a close friend or romantic partner." This, in essence, is closer to the truth. It is also simplified and direct, and you can't get any better than that. Still, I'd like to give it a try. Here is an even simpler and more direct definition: "You are a soul, you need a mate, *so-you'll* mate." Believing that first definition we looked at will have you going in every direction the wind blows you. It might be fun for a short while, but a waste of time the whole while. If you're like me and you once believed, it's okay, look at how far we've come. Celebrate this moment of clarity—you're no longer living in make believe land.

Now I want you to focus on you and quiet your thoughts for a second, just take a moment. I want you to think about your hair. I want you to think about your head, eyes, lips, nose, and ears. I want you to think about your shoulders and neck. I want you to think about your arms, hands, legs, feet and toes. I want you to think about your smile. Now take one deep breath in and one deep breath out. I want you to feel your heartbeat, listen for it, listen to it, and sync yourself to its rhythm. Think of your fondest memory, a time that made you the happiest. Can you hear the laughter? It's always like you remembered it. Now think of the last time you had your favorite dish, maybe even one that your mom used to cook. Can't you smell it, even taste it? Isn't it strange how you are where you are yet you traveled back to places and even smelled or tasted food without moving? This is because you're a human being that has a soul that makes you capable of doing that. You're not just a being of feelings. Feelings aren't facts and are often looking for a place to rent. You're just a human being with a soul who just needs to find a mate. The unfortunate truth is many people miss their game changer because they have the wrong definition in their minds.

RECAP CHAPTER 9:

In Business: When we're distracted, we miss things, especially the things right under our nose. A Game Changer is a newly introduced element or factor that changes an existing situation or activity in a significant way. They have been known to seek you out before there is even a job available. You don't have to put in much work convincing these people of your vision. When a game changer comes along, they can not only see your vision very clearly but also what the missing pieces are.

In Dating: Your Game Changer is a person who might have strong or bright ideas on how you can achieve future personal goals. They see a quality in you that maybe even you don't see. Oftentimes they're right in front of you. Listen young ladies, it would be wise to use your 20s and your beauty to your advantage in finding your life partner, not just living it up. I know girls just want to have fun like the old song says, but at what cost? I'm not saying turn into some gold digger but instead be a goal digger. The same goes for the young gentleman. Having a goal is good, but having a plan to obtain that goal is better. Once we know how our environments use us, then we can understand how to use it to our advantage, especially as single people.

THE APPLICATION:

- Understand that Game Changers know where they are going, with or without you; they just prefer it to be with you.
- Recognize individuals who are vested in your future and keep them close.
- Your youth is supposed to be to your advantage, don't think you have time to waste.
- It's great to have long-term goals, but also have short-term evaluation periods.
- Settling down is and looks different than settling. To settle down is the goal.
- The time you think you have is not promised; the only time you can be certain of is now. Use your time to your advantage.
- Understand there is no soul mate, just other souls who need a mate.

CHAPTER 10

GAME CHANGERS – Part 2

(How I Met My Game Changer)

in dating

Funny truth: for one reason or another, the majority of the married people I know say they didn't like their spouse at first. They can quote the exact reasons why, but then follow it up with some kind of growth statement like, "I wasn't mature" or "I just couldn't see it at the time." The primary culprit for this of course is our blindness to 'types' (Chapter 9) that stem purely from outside-influenced information. This information then reinforces our commitment to a particular mindset, thus causing us to value specific looking people over others. When a person doesn't look like what you've been conditioned to find attractive or drawn to, you may either judge them prematurely or they will fly completely under your radar. That was the case for my wife and I.

When I first met my wife, sparks of a different kind flew. One night, a friend and I decided to attend a charity fundraising gala that our church was sponsoring. We got there early, and as we stood in line, looking suave and debonair, a couple of ladies along with their single guy friend approached us. One of them very confidently said, "Thanks for holding our place in line guys!" That young lady was Elaina Julia Williams, a tall, very outgoing and friendly modelesque beauty. They proceeded to join us, saving themselves a trek to the very back of the now long line. While it was a clever move to her, to me it was a selfish, typical night club tactic, and I didn't like it. I was extremely bothered, and this immediately caused me to put up a guard between us. All I kept saying in my mind was, "You're not getting over on me." I'd already concluded that I didn't need to get to know a person who would do things like that. Although my friend was cool with the idea and invited them to join us, I was admittedly a bit stiff for the rest of the night and my actions supported my feelings. I'm in no way saying that I was right by doing so; in fact, I'm sure my actions cost me the opportunity to get to know her better that night. Had I not acted that way, maybe we would've saved some time.

A few months passed before I saw her again. By this time, we had both become part of a group of friends who often hung out together. Because I'm an observer by nature, I began to really notice her in various interactions and scenarios, and after getting to know her, I understood that her move that first night at the club was really just a part of her personality. I remember thinking of her as a super cool and dope person, nothing more and nothing less. My thoughts and feelings then changed rather quickly. I'd like to share a few very personal journal entries from around that time with you. This will give you a better idea of how easily the shift in my thinking happened and how I approached it.

In this first entry, I was leaving on a business trip to Florida. Here's a disclaimer: I don't know how other people write in their journals, but I like to do it as though I'm telling my close friends a story.

7/2/2014 Wednesday

"Btw...I recently got a new car. It's a pearl white 2012 Nissan Altima Coupe. It's the perfect combination of sporty look and fuel efficiency that I like. I am truly blessed by the blessing. Speaking of which: so I

151

decided that, while I am away, to let my friend Elaina, a girl that's been in my circle of friends for a few months now, hold my car. I knew she had just sold her car and was busing it. And I recently observed how she took great care of another friend's car who had been out of town for months so I felt no hesitation in making the decision. Plus, it's a very convenient way to ensure that you get a ride to and from the airport. Lol!"

While away at the work conference, I had a few personal struggles and wanted to share with someone I trusted. This was my journal entry when I got back to LA:

7/15/2014 Saturday

"So, when Elaina picked me up from the airport and I was taking her back home...I shared some of these things with her. She listened attentively, was understanding and at the end was surprisingly encouraging. And it was at that moment I felt...something. I took in the nature of her entire being and was like "Hmph!" My thoughts: "I'm having a personal conversation, about a real thing, with someone I was not sure I had a close connection with and it feels...cool." Here I was beating myself up about things and here she was telling me that

it's alright. I said I don't want to be that guy dating girl after girl in the church and she said I was so far from being that guy. I liked that.

We talked smoothly on the way to her house and a little longer once we got there. I was assured she was good people from that point on."

She impressed something on me at that moment. She was someone I needed but didn't even know it yet, and I began to process a lot of things following that interaction. This is what happened almost a month later:

8/11/2014 Monday

"After weeks of being cool and laying low, I told Elaina that I liked her and that we should go out and see if anything was there. And if there isn't then we have our friendship regardless. (Not sure why I overlooked her this whole time because we have chilled together in group settings plenty of times. Well, I know why…I was interested in someone else who was my type. But why she started hitting my radar like that is what I'm not sure of. It may have been because we have started serving in the same ministries now and I've gotten to see just how amazing she really is.) Her response though was…she didn't get the same revelation aka no. Not a major blow, it didn't make me feel

one way or the other, I just went back to my regularly scheduled program."

At this point, all I was thinking was, "be bold, put it out there. If you're timid and don't try, you only have yourself to blame." You miss 100% of the shots you don't take. Being bold is your right. If you're bold and miss, it is what it is. It should never take anything away from you. This next entry was only a week later:

8/16/2014 Saturday

"I was on the way up to San Francisco, to help my best friend Cassandra get settled in, and Elaina calls from her job. She calls and tells me she would like to go out with me. I can't lie…I gave the Lord a HUGE SHOUT!!! Lol. And I felt like it was my birthday! Moments before the call I had just prayed that any distractions or veils be lifted from her eyes or the eyes of whomever God has for me so that they might see me in the right way. Wow! God is able. Since I was out of town that weekend and was going to be gone the next weekend as well I told her it would be after I get back. She was cool."

Things were looking up! Let me fast forward to the date:

8/30/2014 Saturday

"E and I go on our date. We had dinner at Firefly, the convo flowed, we saw Guardians of the Galaxy and presumably had a great time. I took her home and on the way we started talking about things going on with her specifically, her situation with another guy she's interested in. I get a sense that she does like me and it could go either way however by the end of the convo I was only confused about why she would be out with me if she liked someone else, especially since we've been talking more. She said I was being so patient with her. So we talked to a peaceful end. I told her I was just going to let her figure things out and chill a bit. I prayed for her knee, since it was hurting and walked her to the door. She said that I was truly amazing (whatever that really means). What's cool is the fact I don't feel like I've had to try with her. With the exception of a couple gestures…buying and giving her a flower to start the date. I felt awkward about that and she seemed awkward about it. I'm not really sure where things go from here."

Honestly, I felt terrible the next day. I woke up feeling rejected, and battled with that feeling for most of the day. I had to make a call to my mentor, Dr. Lovy, and he was able to help me settle my thoughts again. I saw Elaina during the morning church service and at an event later that night. There was only a cordial exchange between us, no great shift happened. I remember wishing I would've stayed home. Let's jump a month and a half ahead from this point:

10/16/2014 Thursday

"When I take the time to start living and enjoying my life a bit I forget to document it lol. E and I have agreed to just be friends. We hung out, went and got ice cream and talked. It was the conclusion she thought was best. I can say I felt the same, but I didn't. However, rather than fight it, and after talking a lil' bit more, I just gave her the Amos 3:3 verse, and we shook hands. I agreed because I'd rather her still feel comfortable around me than awkward or make things awkward. I'm man enough to handle my emotions. I'll be fine. In the midst of it all we have been able to be super chill with each other. No love lost, no regrets. Why? Because I did my part as the man, I put it out there. And we've agreed to be friends. Cool. If anything else were to happen at this point it will have to be led by God and not me. I've prayed about it continually to the point where I'm content whichever way He takes it. Now instead of worrying about things like this when I feel a moment happening, I use that time to just simply pray for my future wife and family. God sees them right now even though I can't and I know He

hears my prayers. I pray my future wife is guided and protected, surrounded by like-minded God-fearing women, that she is spiritually strong, financially blessed, and happy.

Something in me does not believe that Elaina and my story is over. I just feel there is more. Why? Because how I feel about her isn't based on a feeling, but a knowing. I feel drawn. *I've never chosen to have a relationship with anyone building from a friendship level before. Maybe it's my imagination or maybe it's a knowing, I don't know anymore. In the meantime, I just want God to grant me this simple request…and I know He can do it because He is God. The request is…if Elaina is not the one for me to let any of the feelings I have for her not show…better yet, to remove feelings I have for her altogether.*

Better yet…I pray that she finds someone, Amen. Yeah I know it all seems drastic, but I didn't ask for this and I don't want to deal with it longer than necessary. Our friendship will be enough. This is also where things have been a little confusing for her, in her not being able to think about me in any other capacity. Only God knows the rest of our stories."

As I reflect on the journey, I recognize that although it's not easy to go down memory lane at times, all of life's lessons are good lessons. Let's move forward, now that we've taken a deep dive into my real-life journal entries and the genesis of my experiences with my wife—oh yeah, you heard me correctly, I got the girl! She now has my last name, lives in a house I bought her, and is the mother of my children. Our days together only keep getting better and better with time. I wonder, despite our rocky start, did you notice who the game changer was? Let me cut right to it. Although I would definitely credit my wife as being my game changer because of the way she has impacted my quality of life and standards, I was in fact hers first. I saw things in her she did not see and focused only on those things, and I included myself in plans and goals she had whether she liked it at the time or not. She went on a mission trip and I knew she wouldn't have much money while gone, so I found a way to support her at separate times. I would send $500 here and $500 there as a donation. It was very innate in me; I just wanted to see her thrive in life.

As I stated earlier, game changers often experience rejection before promotion. I would like to also point out that regardless of the rejection, game changers stay in motion. A word of advice for you: always stay moving forward or upward. Let people find you better than when they last saw you. It is important that you never stop being someone of and with high value. The value you carry is how you will ultimately be measured.

RECAP CHAPTER 10:

In Dating: When someone doesn't look like you've been conditioned to find attractive, you judge them prematurely or they will fly completely under your radar.

THE APPLICATION:

Men: Be assertive—ask for the date. "Let's go out to see if anything is there." If nothing's there, cool. Maybe the connection will serve a different purpose down the road.

Women: Be mentally available. Don't prejudge the person. Be willing to let things naturally unfold.

- Being bold is your right. If you're bold and miss, it just is what it is.
- Understand that rejection gives direction. When you get a "no" you should still know where to go.
- Always keep moving forward. Let people find you better than they last saw you.

CHAPTER 11

TALK OF INVESTMENT

(Guard Your Heart)

This is a very important chapter. I was uncertain where I would place it in the book, but knew it had to be included. There are 3 types of people you will encounter as CEO, and you must be able to recognize them: the right partners, potential investors, and those who only talk of investment. The right partner will be a natural investor and seek to truly enhance Your Life, Inc. in every way. At this point, we've been able to identify them as Game Changers. They come in many forms—young, old, short, tall, with lots of experience and little capital, with lots of capital and little experience, or with great ideas that can raise capital. The potential investors usually have a substantial amount of capital and are only looking for ways to diversify their portfolio, get a return, and increase their profits and net worth. Then you have those who only talk of investment. Such people may have access to capital, know the lingo, but solely want free or insider information for their benefit without making any real investment in your company. In other words, they know from the start that their intentions are not to invest, but you unfortunately won't know until after you've given them the benefit of the doubt and time is wasted. It happens all the time. Let's look at why you would be talking to investors in the first place, shall we? The reasons can vary from simply needing more capital, wanting to expand a business, or wanting to sell a business.

IN BUSINESS

Oftentimes, investors will want to do their due diligence before making any permanent financial decisions. This may require several sit downs or video conference meetings, and polite requests to look at your company's proprietary financial information. On the surface this could all seem like nothing more than the talk of investment, but it's different because the talk of investment is just that—talk—and it will always cost you in some way to entertain it. All these actions are wise and make perfect sense to do. Before you commit any capital to anything you should definitely know how long it would take you to get a return on your investment. I fully subscribe to this plan of action.

Depending on your immediate need, however, you may want to hold off on releasing any financials for as long as possible. You should have meetings with potential investors and seek to fully understand their business and reason of interest in your business. This is especially true if they came out of nowhere. If it is you that sought them out, there is a slight aspect change, but it is nevertheless still important to follow this principle. Let's say the investors sought you out. It would be your job to also probe into them as much as they probe into your company. I've noticed that people often fantasize when it comes to details; the less they know, the happier they are. I sincerely hope you don't think like this. Personally, I love asking people the hard questions, not because I want them to think I'm a difficult person, but that I'm not too easy. And admittedly, I'm not. The saying, "people take the path of least resistance," is indicative of the notion that people want what is easy. Don't be easy, and don't be afraid to ask questions.

If the investors sought you out, it means you have something they want. Maybe your business model is amazing; or perhaps it's your location. Either way, you hold some cards and should use that to your advantage. If you sought them out, however, most likely it's because you need them more than they need you. And if that is the case, they may toy with you a bit depending on the seriousness of your timeframe. In other words, how mission-critical is it that you sought them out? Are you in need of fresh eyes and perspective for your company? Are you tired of doing things alone? Or are you going bankrupt without the extra cash?

DON'T BE ANXIOUS

After owning my business and working in the same industry for over ten years, I was ready to make a change. I didn't see a possibility for more growth for myself doing the same thing, plus I was just tired. So, I decided to reach out to a corporate resource division that handles sales and acquisitions. A few weeks went by, and then a vetted lead of someone who was potentially interested in buying my company came my way. The first meeting was over the phone, and the investor really brought the charm and intrigue to the table as he asked all the right questions. We connected as we spoke, throwing around a few "bro" this or that, ended the meeting on a positive note and scheduled time to talk in person in about a week. When the day came, hours before the meeting I received a message explaining he would be unable to meet physically but could jump on another call. I was fine with that, and the second meeting went equally well. He asked me more in-depth questions about the day-to-day operations of the business, then asked if he could see the proprietary financial information. Because I was eager to sell the company and move on, I was fully accommodating. Moreover, I was sold on the fact that our business models complemented each other perfectly. At this point, he was vetted, seemed really interested, and his business would benefit from acquiring the service offerings my business offered; it appeared to be a match made. It seemed to me like an easy-to-close transaction and that the feeling was mutual. We ended the call on the note that I would send over some of the information he had requested and that we would finally meet in person the following week. This was pre-Covid so there was no apprehension at all about it. I sent the information immediately after our call and went into the weekend hopeful and happy.

The following week, I reached out to him on the day of the meeting to make sure he had all the correct details. He, in turn, let me know that we'd have to push the meeting back because he was out of town. Still hopeful, I agreed to reschedule for the end of the following week. When the day came, however, I never heard from the guy, and never heard from him after that. It was later explained to me by someone in the sales and acquisition department that it isn't uncommon for an investor, although vetted, to only be interested in learning the ins and outs of how the business works, and find it cheaper to do so by entertaining talks rather than commit. It is assumed that they then copy the model and start a similar business or service themselves.

Even though I learned the incident wasn't uncommon, for me it was demoralizing. I had already put my hope in the future sale, or at least, adding a partner, and on top of that, I had really believed the other person would keep their word. It felt personal, and I took it as such. *Wait a minute, I took business personal?* Yep, this is the cardinal sin and I committed it! In all my years I had other experiences that should've prepared me for that, but my restlessness overrode all conditioning; so much so, that after a short period of time had passed and another investor popped up, the same thing happened again! This really put me in a dry place mentally and made me view things on a personal level. At the time, it was hard for me to separate myself from my business successes and failures. I tied so much of my identity into my business' value and performance that it was hard to move on if others didn't see or value my business the same way I did. The important lesson that came from this was realizing that I was not my business entity and its value wasn't a personal reflection of me. However, Your Life, Inc. must be able to weather the ebbs and flows of life that will come. This still doesn't mean you need to take losses personally; you should neither take wins nor losses personally. Once you agree with the fact that everything you experience lasts temporarily (whether good, bad, or otherwise), then you will see your losses as lessons learned and know how to make your wins more worthwhile. What I perceived as a loss was indeed very temporary, and later, I ended up selling my company to a bigger, more resourceful corporation than simply a personal investor. This proved to me just how valuable my business was, and taught me that all amazing things take time.

in dating

Just as in business, the talk of investment happens in dating all the time. People often talk about having a life together, but it doesn't mean they will deliver on their talk. Talk is cheap and costs nothing, while actions are the true currency of accomplishments. Potential suitors pop up all the time just to fade away, and yet, sadly, many get excited by potential partners due to their yearning for a relationship. They make promises and they break promises, along with breaking hearts.

When you are too anxious for something, or in this case, someone, the majority of the time it is a sign that you're not truly ready for what you say you want after all. Notice I said truly ready, not truly wanting it. We all want what we want, that is our right. Readiness, however, is different. If you're easily moved (emotionally) by the words or actions of people toward you then they are your remote control. Learn to not be easily moved, and most importantly, not to be anxious. Here is a tip for you: When you're least anxious about having something that you want, that's when you're most ready to receive it.

Perhaps you've been single for a while and you're tired of it—I get it. You feel left behind as the people closest to you are either getting engaged, married or have started families, and you feel the pressure to make that part of your life happen. Trust me, I get it, it's annoying. Not only do you want it for yourself so badly, but now your identity, your successes and failures seem to be tied to whether 'this' happens or not. You want someone to see you and want to spend time with you. I've been there. It sometimes feels like a dark and lonely place that can easily weigh on you. Hear me when I tell you this, give all those things no attention. I repeat, don't let your emotions get the best of you; let them know you're the boss. If not, you'll have to fight with desperation, and try to prove to yourself that *you're desired*, which won't be an easy fight. It will have you ready to settle just to say you 'accomplished' something but in reality, you just wanted to shut up the people closest to you who shared their opinions at one point. I know your desire is heavy, but be careful, don't settle. If it's your desire to get married and have a family, don't just settle for having a kid and a relationship with someone. Sure, it will feel progressive for a moment but without the right foundation, nothing of value will truly stand. Don't allow people to cause you to settle in this way. I want to say something that's a little direct but all the way true. Are you ready? Ok here goes, "NOBODY CARES ABOUT YOU!" Wow! That sounds harsh right? Well, it's not, and let me tell you why.

NOBODY CARES ABOUT YOU

In the beginning, whether it's your parents, siblings, cousins, aunties, uncles—you name it—everyone will know how to make you feel seen, heard, and loved. If you get sick, need some money or food, or even advice, you can rely on these people. Your friends will also have special value to you. They may call you when they go out and see if you want to join, if you need a ride, they're happy to come pick you up, or if the day is free, they might just want to kick it with you. After all, if you have nothing else to do then you might as well be around people you like being around, right? Life is precious and feels the most rewarding during these moments. What happens next, however, is remarkable. There comes a certain point in your life where it seems that all the people who love you most have very little time for you. It didn't start this way, so what happened? People's lives, interests and priorities begin to change a bit, and things have to change in order to survive. Jobs, career, family, and paying taxes, rent or mortgage all take center stage of our lives and become the priority. We've all now joined a club.

What you may not notice is that along the way, while the gradual change was happening, you were shifted out of a few clubs. A club is an association or organization dedicated to a particular interest or activity, and all clubs have their own language. We form clubs knowingly and unknowingly with people all the time, it's one of the most natural things we do with one another. We do this while change continuously happens all around us.

Let's look at single people for example, specifically single men, and let's say they are part of The Bro Club. The Bro Club consists of single guys who do single guy things like partying, hanging out, and getting girls' numbers. At one point in life, most single guys all have The Bro Club in common. Then as time passes, a few get girlfriends and start The Bros in Relationships Club. Consequently, the relationship between The Bros and The Bros in Relationships naturally shifts. They no longer have 'getting girls' numbers' in common, so they just become guys who might party or hang out together. Now, imagine out of The Bros in Relationships Club a few get engaged, and create The Engaged

Guys Club. The relationship between The Bros in Relationships and The Engaged Guys naturally shifts again; they're not just guys with girlfriends anymore, they're now gentlemen with fiancées. They can still get together, hang out and talk about guy stuff, but they might not party together any more. Although they may talk about general relationship stuff, they now prefer to discuss the topic with people on their level. Out of The Engaged Guys Club, some get married before others and create the Husbands With Wives Club. They're no longer gentlemen with fiancées, they have become husbands. At this level, although they might hang out with people not belonging to this club, their different understanding and dynamic of relationships will usually cause them to want to hang out with those most like themselves. Men who are married don't benefit from hanging out with single guys who are only focused on getting girls. Single guys who want to get married, however, greatly benefit from the relationship advice of married men.

Regardless of all the shifts that have happened, the one thing they have carried in common and that hasn't changed the entire time, is that they're men. While this is the key to belonging to the different clubs, this is unfortunately where it also gets tricky.

If a guy who is still in The Bro Club doesn't recognize the shifts that happen and the different clubs that exist at different levels, he will try to interact with a husband as if they are in the same club and not understand why the exchange is less favorable. For example, if a bro calls a husband and tries to treat him like a bro, asking to hang out, the husband will most likely decline because of his different set of priorities. If the bro disregards the club shift and takes the decline personally, he might then perceive the husband as the problem or the one acting differently, which in turn might cause some unnecessary strife in that relationship. So, although all men will always be able to relate to one another on some level, with each club a man enters there will be different rules and regulations that must be observed.

I just went through that long explanation to tell you this: **a person's interest in their own progression will necessitate leaving the interests (or clubs) of others behind**. Though it may feel personal to those you leave, always remember, it's just business, it's just Your Life, Inc. We are innately tribal and have a strong need to belong to groups with common interests. The saying, "your life goes in the direction of the five people closest to you," is true. This is because you become the sounding board of the thoughts, opinions, and perspectives of your peers. When your peers share strategies and grand ideas, it often naturally causes you to measure them against your personal life; you reassess a few of your own decisions and then you start to naturally adjust where necessary. I call these healthy relationships, and we all need these types of relationships. I've discovered over time, being around people you've formed healthy relationships with causes you to desire and achieve higher levels.

Remember these two simple rules: Firstly, always know someone *is* more successful than you, and secondly, always know someone more successful than you. If you always know someone *is* more successful than you it causes you to be less jealous and threatened, and instead more inspired by them. It also allows you to give yourself a mental break as you'll be less concerned with their success and more focused on yours. You won't kill yourself trying to be the "first-to-do" something, because most likely you won't be. We all stand on the shoulders of giants. Anything that will be created already exists in some form. Your unique insight will serve you better in bringing some freedom to the innovation needed to continue to move things forward. When you know someone is more successful than you, you can chill and see your journey as its own going forward.

If you always *know* someone more successful than you, it allows you to have access to a proven mind or their proven model for your benefit. You have someone who can guide you if needed, step by step through rough terrain and onto the higher plains of advancement. When you have someone in your life more successful than you, it allows you to also set a bar in your mind of what's possible and take the necessary steps in achieving it. Personally, I live by the motto "if you can shake their hand, you can do what they can." This is my bridge of understanding that all things are possible. Grant it, the literal handshaking part is metaphorical, but the mindset part however is literal. In order to impact things, you need a vision or someone to help you realize it. With the vision identified it's only a matter of time until you obtain it. How you see the world determines how you are to impact it. I see the business models in everything I do which causes me to see things as a product or service. I know that can make me sound a bit cynical but it's just how I see the world. Fortunately for you, we have this masterpiece of literature because of it.

Understanding these things brings me back to the "Nobody cares about you" statement I made earlier. Do I really mean the people in your life don't care about or love you? No, of course not. I'm sure many are concerned over your well-being. The point I am making however is "you're supposed to care about yourself" in such a way that you're too busy to notice what other people are doing. This isn't permission to be selfish and treat people as less than, no. It's the opposite. It's permission to love and appreciate yourself so much that you're not just viewing life as how it impacts you but how you can impact life. It's treating yourself so well that the way you treat others mirrors your personal care. It's taking the time to be so healthy mentally, physically and even spiritually that your only expectations of people or from people is no expectation at all. It's going after your desires. It's seeing people in the right light and knowing who is for you. When you care about and value yourself the right way, the more things will seem less like they're happening to you and more like they're happening for you.

RECAP CHAPTER 11:

In Business: You have to be able to recognize the difference between 3 types of people: the right partners, potential investors and people who only talk of investment. Someone with only the talk of investment may have access to capital and know the lingo, but solely want free or insider information for their benefit without making any real investment in your company. In other words, they'll know from the start that their intentions are not to invest, but you unfortunately won't know until after you've given them the benefit of the doubt and your time was wasted. Your company must be able to weather the ebbs and flows of life that will come. This still doesn't mean you need to take losses personally. You should neither take wins nor losses personally. Once you agree with the fact that everything you experience only lasts temporarily (whether good, bad or otherwise) then you will see your losses as lessons learned and know how to make your wins more worthwhile.

In Dating: Talk is cheap and costs nothing; actions are the true currency of accomplishments. Potential suitors pop up all the time just to fade away. They make promises and they break promises, along with breaking hearts. Many get excited by potential partners due to their yearning for a relationship. If you're easily moved (emotionally) by the words or actions of people towards you then they are your remote control. Learn to not be easily moved, and most importantly, not to be anxious. The best indicator that you're ready for something is actually when you really don't want it. You're supposed to care about yourself, and in such a way that you're too busy to notice what other people are doing.

THE APPLICATION:

- Don't be easy, and don't be afraid to ask questions when talking to potential investors.
- Take neither wins nor losses personally. Everything you experience is temporary.
- Talk is cheap. Your actions are the true currency of your accomplishments.
- Always know there is someone more successful than you and always know someone more successful than you.

CHAPTER 12

THE FIRING

(The Letting Go)

I'd like to give you a gift, the gift of clarity. I find that transparency helps us connect best with information, and my main goal with this project is to be as straightforward as possible. If you choose to listen to me and apply these principles, you will experience great improvement not only in your company, but in the company you keep as well. It truly doesn't get any more straightforward than that. Having said that, it's important for you to understand there is an exception to everything we've learned. Robert Greene, the author of one of my favorite books and a flawless piece of art, in "The 48 Laws of Power" establishes that with each law there is a *reversal*. Reversals are simply instances in which the exception or opposite to the rule can also be true. In this chapter, we will examine some exceptions.

It benefits you nothing to want change in an area of your life but not know how to attain it. Should you choose to use the keys

179

I've given you in this book, they will unlock many doors and cause you to reach greater heights of achievement and prosperity in both your business ventures and your relationship desires.

This book is to serve as no more than that mirror you look at before you leave your home. It is meant to reveal your blind spots. When you look at your reflection, it's important to acknowledge what you actually see and not lie to yourself. It's up to you to observe the information the mirror gives you and decide if you like what you're reflecting. Taking note of our reflection is vital as it is the only thing that allows us to get a glimpse of what the rest of the world may actually see. That which the world doesn't see or know about us we reveal in our interactions; but the issue is, we can't truly trust our actions all of the time. This is due to the fact that they've been compromised by all the influences and information we've stored up since childhood. It's only right, then, that as we grow and mature, we learn how to reexamine what we know and how it affects us as we strive to make better decisions for our lives.

IN BUSINESS

The Rule: It's Not Good To Get Fired
Reversal 1: Not all firings are bad

You can fire people or you can get fired. Whatever side you fall on, the truth is, both suck. Yet, they're all a part of life. Even though you can have greatly documented reasons, one of the toughest decisions you can make is to fire someone. Not everyone may have experienced that, but I have. It's a tough thing to do, even if the employee wasn't cutting it. If you've never had to fire someone, good for you. Have you ever been fired though? Not a great feeling either, right? It doesn't matter how much you wanted to pretend you liked your job, the day you're informed that you won't be coming back to work can be devastating. Why? Because when something is unexpected, it typically means we're not prepared for it. Who likes to be blindsided? I doubt anyone prepares to be fired, just like you don't plan to have to fire. In both cases, you must learn to accept it and move on.

Here are a few questions to answer that will help make firing, although tough, just a little easier:

- Are they lazy? (What are their real goals?)

- Do they show enthusiasm for their work and the company?

- Are the results there, do they produce well?

- Are they punctual?

- Do they increase morale in the office or stifle it?

- What do their co-workers really think about them?

- Do they have or show a bad attitude?

- Is it time to just move on?

- Are they not the right fit because they just belong somewhere else?

These are important questions to answer because to fire someone really translates to changing someone's life, for the good or bad. How can it be good? Well, very insightful bosses can usually see if someone is limiting themselves or being held back by the job. In such a case, the firing intervenes as some may say fate would, and sends them on a path to find their true destiny. I once knew a pastor who was fired from his high-paying corporate America job because his boss knew he was holding himself back—they actually told him that. As devastating as it may have seemed, just a few short years later he moved to North Carolina, started an amazing Bible-based church and today has a thriving ministry. His firing led to bigger and better things.

I WAS FIRED ONCE

About 13 years ago, I was hired to work for an AT&T corporate store as an Assistant Manager to manage sales reps. By this time in my life, I had already worked 3 years in a whole other industry as General Manager, so I had quite a few years' experience managing people. This, however, turned out to be the only thing these two jobs had in common — the management of people. I struggled for a few months because I knew nothing about the mobile phone industry, but I had enough management experience to rely on and get by. At the time my ego was too big to admit that I needed the help and those sales reps tested me big time. To put it plainly, it looked bad, and I'm pretty certain I affected morale. Here, I was at the busiest location in the region, with a great boss, making great money, and yet I wasn't pulling my weight. By the time I had figured out what I was doing, the decision was made to transfer me to another, slower location. This also changed my commute to work from a 10-minute (4 mile) drive to a 32-minute (25 mile) drive.

Once I got to the new location, although I was able to handle my old problems better, I now had brand new problems. At this store, I had a very lazy boss who didn't want to do her job. In fact, she wanted me to do her job. One time she told me she was leaving early, after we opened at 9am. I was fine with it, but when I asked at what time she planned on leaving, she told me 9:30am. This was not due to an emergency; in fact, it was something she did quite often. My last boss at the previous store once told me the same thing during a 9 to 6pm shift, and when I asked him the time he was leaving, he said 5:30pm. I later found out it was because she lived less than 10 minutes away and knew she could rush back whenever the regional bosses came in. I became vocal about it, and I wanted to speak up for the other employees who felt berated and mistreated. Let's just say it wasn't long afterward that I was fired and the higher ups fired her too. That was the first and last time I have ever been fired. However, the truth is, those things didn't happen to me, they happened for me. I didn't belong there; I was aiming too low and it was apparent. Not even 8 months later, I packed up my car, drove 2,642 miles and moved to Los Angeles, California, the 2nd largest city in the United States. 10 years later I can honestly say I have made it here. This has by far been my greatest adventure yet; life has turned out amazing for me and I'm still going. Getting fired became my reason to try a new approach toward my life, even though it didn't feel like it at the time.

in dating

The Rule: It's Not Good To Be Broken Up With
Reversal 2: Not all breakups are bad

Sometimes you break up with people, and other times you get broken up with. While both can be devastating, they are also a necessary part of life. There are numerous reasons to break up with someone, and regardless of whether those reasons are good or bad, it's still tough to do. If you're reading this and have yet to experience that, good for you; not everyone has, but most will. No matter which side you're on—breaking up or getting broken up with—it comes with a cost, the main cost being its effect on your routine. Parting ways in relationships can be difficult, and most try to avoid it because as creatures of habit, our dependency on them makes us less equipped to handle random or sudden changes in our day-to-day lives. If I'm completely honest, I've always viewed breaking up with someone as being emotionally the same as coping with the death of a loved one. This is especially true when you are the one left behind. Whatever the case, you have to cope with your life going on without them and your time together only living in your memories. Unlike death however, someone deciding to live their life without you seems harder to understand. Have you ever ended a relationship with someone before? Chances are, you didn't feel this way because you validated all your reasons before you had to do it. To the person on the receiving end of that break up, however, a bus just hit them. It's not a great feeling. It doesn't matter if the writing was on the wall or not, an unexpected change is still an unexpected change. No matter the coping method, it's important to know how to move on.

Here are a few questions to answer that will help make breaking up with someone, although tough, just a little easier:

- Do we have any real purpose together?
- Are they adding any value to my life?

- Do they show enthusiasm for their future as well as our future?

- Are the results there, do they produce well?

- Are they attentive to me or self-absorbed?

- Overall, do my friends and family like them? What do the people who know me best think of our relationship?

- What do their friends and family really think about me?

- Do they have or show a bad attitude?

- Is it just time to move on?

- Are we a good fit?

- Do we just belong with other people?

These are important questions to answer because to break up with someone means it changes two people's lives, for good or bad. How can it be good? Because sometimes people just belong with other people. One of the problems people create for themselves is still being emotionally attached with those who they are no longer with. It doesn't matter how many memories you created with someone, holding on to what you should clearly let go of will only cause you pain. Break ups are destiny once again making sure you stay in the flow of life and in the direction it's taking you. Since we've already established previously what a soulmate is and isn't, understand that letting go of people is the best thing you can do. There are plenty of good-looking people searching for love in this world. I suppose Disney did do something right in one of their movies, when the character sang repeatedly, "Let it go, let it go!" When you accept that change is here to help you, you grow. I know countless people whose relationships ended and the very next person who came into their life was Mr. or Mrs. Right. Letting go of people usually leads to receiving better people.

IN BUSINESS

The Rule: When You Quit, You Fail
Reversal 3: You Make Better Decisions By Not Being Afraid To Make Bad Ones

Contrary to what many would say, quitting is not a negative thing in itself. Quitting can only be negative when it's decided from a place of emotion instead of a place of careful assessment. What do I mean? If you quit something (say your job) because you had a bad day, it's probably not a well thought out decision and you most likely did not factor in all of your responsibilities. However, if you've been sitting with the thought of quitting for a while, weighed your pros and cons, and secured other options, then quitting may be the best thing to do.

Oftentimes people would probably try to give you general advice when it pertains to quitting, thinking they're doing you a favor. While their intentions may be good, you must still do your own inner work to know if you're making the right decision. How can you do this? By asking yourself these questions:

• Is there any more room for growth in this current place I'm in?

• Is this the very best I can do for myself?

• Is now the right time to go? If not now, when?

• How do I really feel about what I'm doing everyday?

• Am I valued as much as I would like to be? Can I change that?

• How long have I been thinking about leaving?

• If I stay, will anything change?

There's a saying, "It's better to measure ten times and cut once than to cut once and measure ten times." In other words, be sure of what you're sure of. This is a popular proverb, and while the author is unknown, this is sage advice meant to make one better at decision making, a very important element in business.

It's important that we assess and understand our personal limits. When we know what we lack, we can better know what we need. You shouldn't fear not knowing something nor making bad decisions, because both help you to grow; being indecisive can cause people not to grow. Sometimes the best way to become better at making good decisions is by having made bad ones. This of course doesn't mean you should reject or accept all advice when it's given to you, but rather, that you yourself should know where it best fits based on your situation and all you've considered.

ONCE A QUITTER ALWAYS A QUITTER

This is true but not in the way you might think. Earlier I shared how in my teens I left one job for another, then another, then another after that. This happened because I was always willing to let go of one thing in order to obtain a better thing. Over the years my reasoning for this became stronger and stronger because the filter through which I processed decisions honestly was void of emotion and full of much needed facts. When I went

190

off to college and walked onto the football team, it seemed all my goals were obtainable. By the time I was a Junior, I even entertained the idea of one day trying out for the NFL. Afterall, I was a pretty good athlete at the time. I was 21 years old, six feet tall, 185 pounds, with a 4.56 seconds 40 yd dash, 33-inch vertical jump, 10-foot standing broad jump, 365-pound bench max and could rep 225 pounds 14 times. After a couple of summer camps, and proving myself, it looked like I was finally about to get the shot I was after—playing time and being 1 or 2 on the free safety depth chart. However, at the height of it all, I pulled my hamstring twice and it never felt the same afterwards. Although I knew I had what it took to play, my heart and the time I had left before graduating told me it would be better to focus on having an amazing student academic life and leave the student athletic life behind.

When I told my position coach, however, his advice to me was, "If you quit football now, you'll quit everything else for the rest of your life." His words resonated greatly because of the respect I had for him, which caused me to doubt my decision as well as my own personal assessment. I didn't want to be a quitter of the things that lay ahead in my unknown future. It almost felt like a curse to me. So, what did I do? I listened to the coach. For an entire season I sat on the sidelines hoping things in my mind would change, but they didn't. The longer I stayed, the more it felt like I had made the wrong decision. Once the season was over and I had the option to come back I decided not to. I was told that if I came back, things would be better for me and it would be my time to shine, but I'd already determined that I didn't want to shine in that way anymore. I had already assessed that less than 1% would have a shot of trying out for the NFL combine and even less than that would make it. Instead, for the first time in 4 years, I only focused on my academics and excelled in my GPA the remaining semesters.

My coach's advice wasn't wrong, he just had the wrong person. The reality was that he was projecting his fear onto me, as most people do to others. I believe that if he were to ever quit football, he would not find much purpose outside of it and would continue to quit everything else for the rest of his life. In fact, after all these years later, he is still a football coach. Football is life for him, but it was never life for me, only an activity. I moved on and became a businessman who watches an occasional NFL game whenever I happen to catch one. I've never been a quitter, but I've always been an assessor. Whenever someone gives you advice, and you have enough living experiences to draw from, assess your life first and see if their advice fits your situation. The sooner you assess your life, the sooner you can quit the things that are occupying your time.

in dating

The Rule: Always Think Highly of Yourself
Reversal 4: You May Not Yet Be Who You Think You Are

Take off the 'thinking highly of yourself' hat and put it down for just a second. Now, pick up the facts about yourself. I say 'facts' because I recognize that some people struggle with self-esteem issues, but those are internal perceptions about oneself, not facts. Now that you have your facts hat on, are you an Eager Dater, a Time-Waster, The One Everybody Wants or God's Gift to Someone? Remember what I said earlier in the book—all of these can change. You could be at any one of these stages at any time, each producing its own rewards once you advance to the next. But which one are you right now?

Not everyone is who they think they are and ready for what they say they desire. It's easy for anyone to say they want what they currently don't have; but being ready for those things is something different altogether. How do you know you're truly ready for what you want? That's easy; it's when you're willing to do what it takes to make it happen. With all things, whether in business or in dating, you have to show a *proof of concept*. Proof of concept is the tangible example of turning a concept into a reality. To *say* you want a companion or life partner is always easier to do than to *show* that proof of concept. The key thing in dating is to always show the necessary effort it requires. What is your proof of concept? Have you put forth or applied the effort to carry out the specific things you want to accomplish in and for your life?

In other words:

- How are you demonstrating you want what you say you are ready for?
- What relationship experiences do you have, whether good, bad or indifferent, that you're ready to apply as a guide to help you obtain new romantic opportunities?

This is where being honest with ourselves serves us best. Let's forget wanting to have a companion for a second, and instead examine 'why':

- Why do you want a companion? Is it because you're lonely? Sorry, not strong enough.

- Is it in order to have a family? That's great, but why do you desire to have a family?

- Why should someone want to start a family with you? Is it because you're good looking and you'd produce beautiful kids? Sorry, looks fade with time. Is it because you have a great job and can financially take care of some things? Sorry, job statuses are fickle and ever changing; look no further than our most recent example, the Pandemic of 2020.

Your reasons have to be examined, and frankly speaking, they ought to be solid. You could be wondering, what if the reasons mentioned are my exact reasons? To that I would say, it's better to know thyself and where you are than to lie to thyself. If these are in fact your reasons for wanting a companion, then it would be wise to also embrace the fact that you need to build stronger reasons.

PUT ME IN COACH

I once coached a very reserved and introverted gentleman in courting a young lady. I knew them both, but they did not know each other personally. They were both single and had shared with me separately their desire to find a companion and get married. From my perspective, they both had areas of opportunity that the other could help with. The only thing I could do was bring them together, but they would have to discover this for themselves. They were not 'unequally yoked' either, as the Bible says. On paper, they had a 1-to-2-year age difference, Masters Degrees, and were both career-focused. However, she was thriving in her career while he was still trying to make it in his. One day, as I was speaking with the gentleman about the young lady and helping him understand the basic premise of this book, he asked me, "Am I a Game Changer (God's Gift To Someone)?" I looked him square in the eye and told him, "No." Not because he can't or won't be, but because he, at the time, wasn't. I elected to keep him grounded by telling him the truth.

The truth was, although they had a lot in common, he, unlike her at the time, did not use the momentum of the years of school to build a budding career for himself. After getting his Master's Degree, he changed his career goals and went in a slightly different direction. He began to pursue his dreams in

Hollywood, and at the age 37 at the time, didn't quite have anything to show for his pursuits thus far. He was very resourceful, but also didn't have a steady job; my man just needed some guidance and focus. I told him he was more like a small company. When you're a single man, in your mid to late thirties, with not much to show for it, it can cause your company to be less desired. He needed to get the business plan together and attract an investor. If he didn't take time to prepare for what he desired, it would be nothing more than a wish.

Listen, if you're a single man or woman who wants to go after your dreams, great, do that; but understand that for everything you get, there is something you exchanged for it. Life will always require sacrifices and exchanges. A dream comes with many costs, oftentimes the things we desire most. It's not impossible to have it all, so long as you prepare for it. In his case, he needed to prepare mentally, physically, emotionally and financially for his family life to manifest. As much as he wanted a family, he hadn't been preparing his lifestyle for it. She, on the other hand, was well put together, very efficient, and successful. On her own, she was definitely like a Fortune 500 company, or in other words, a Game Changer. However, mentality wise, she was too much in her own way to see his potential as a candidate

197

and hers as a company. She actually wanted someone more like a Top Recruit who wouldn't leave, but we both know that would've just faded away.

I thought she would see herself as more of a Game Changer to his small company and figure it out and make boss moves. It may have been too much for me to expect, but I thought she would clearly see the components he was missing and what she could add to his life. That's all he needed actually, the right partner and a little investment. On his part, he was more of an Eager Dater at the time, but he was also very coachable; all he needed was the right investor to take a chance on him. Under the right circumstances, he will progress very quickly to Game Changer status. He is definitely on his way to becoming a top CEO, and the unfortunate truth is that, when he gets his stuff together, he will be able to attract any top-level woman. For women, it's not that easy. I'm not subscribing to the whole 'shelf-life' or 'biological clock' concept, but rather to the simple fact that in the world I know, men are the ones who hold the key to marriage. It's the men who propose, not women. And of course, I'm speaking traditionally. I know of cases where the reverse happened, but they didn't last long. Even though society is steadily changing, this is still the reality.

RECAP CHAPTER 12:

In Business: You can fire people or you can get fired. Whatever side you fall on, the truth is both suck, yet, they're all a part of life. Even though you can have greatly documented reasons, one of the toughest decisions you can make is to fire someone. I doubt anyone prepares to be fired, just like you don't plan to have to fire. In both cases, you must learn to accept it and move on.

The Reversal: No matter what you experience, you're moving toward your destiny.

In Dating: Sometimes you break up with people and other times you get broken up with, both can be devastating but also a necessary part of life. There are numerous reasons to break up with someone, whether good or bad it's still tough to do. In fact, I've always understood breaking up with someone to be emotionally the same as coping with the death of a loved one. This is especially true when you are the one left behind. In both cases, you have to cope with your life going on without them and your time together only living in memories. The Reversal: No matter what, you're making room for your destiny partner.

THE APPLICATION:

- End things on your own terms or come to terms when things end.

- Assess your life and situations often; use wisdom at all times.

- Make sure the advice from others toward you isn't their projected fears in disguise.

- Prepare for what you want; it's the only way to truly know that you're ready for it.

- Be honest with where you are; grow by doing the work. (Don't pretend you're a Game Changer when you're still an Easy Hire and don't pretend you're a Fortune 500 company when you're still a small company.)

- Pay the cost to be the boss. Be who you think you are. (Set the goals for what you want, write them down, and go get it.)

THE FINAL CHAPTER

PAY THE COST TO BE THE BOSS

I remember, as a young child, whenever I would get tired of being treated like a kid or not being taken seriously, and would challenge my parents, my mom would say, "You gotta pay the cost to be the boss!" And my reply to that would be, "How much is it?" Not sure I remember the moments after that but hey, I made it, I'm still alive! I was always genuinely intrigued by the idea of independence and what it took to be in charge. I wasn't a bad kid by any stretch of the imagination, I just wanted to know what it would take to change the things I felt needed to be changed. While I recognized I was under my parents' care for a good reason, a part of me secretly knew it wouldn't be for long. I wish my parents understood at that time that what I was really saying was, "I have a zest for life and I know that it has a greater purpose." Of course, it didn't help that this zest for life got me in trouble more than a few times at school too.

A part of me believes that they did know this but just didn't know what to do with it. Growing up my parents would often tell me the story of how a good family friend, who was a rather successful entrepreneur, looked over at me when I was barely 3 years old and said, "That kid is going to make it, and people are going to be borrowing money from him one day." It changed my life. Ever since the day I heard this story, I've been in pursuit of that 'one day'. I believed it with all my heart. I didn't know how it would happen, but I knew that no matter what, after it had all been said and done, I was going to be successful, I was going to be in charge, and I was going to be a boss.

I set my sights on being a boss very early in life and it indeed has cost me. In the early days, it cost me friends and being understood. I've always been the loner in the group, and not much has really changed with that. I was never like a kid when I was a kid, because I always thought about actions and their consequences, and sought after wisdom from elders. Each decade of my life was more of the same. People around me often said I was too intense or uptight, and while they were not all wrong, they never tried to understand why. I've never looked at life as a joke or taken it lightly, and that has cost me in a few areas. I forfeited a lot of youthful fun because I thought they were pointless.

I also became a father in my mid-twenties, something that I credit to this day as being one of the best things to ever happen to me. Why? Because it gave me a sobering perspective on life— that life is not perfect, I'm not perfect, people are not perfect, and things happen. Everything we go through will come back to aid us later. Although my pursuits have not always been understood, and regardless of what others say, I've always been true to myself, my pace, my life, and my journey. The road has been bright some days and lonely other days, but I always knew I would win in the end. I always knew I would see the best days, and I always knew that one day I would finally be that boss that I paid the cost to become. **Sacrifice is the cost you pay to be the boss.** It's a hefty price but guess what…it's WORTH IT!

I truly want to see you win, and the biggest thing you can do for yourself is to always be honest with who you see in the mirror. Always know where you stand. As this book comes to a close, use this information again and again to help someone else. You are now the possessor of wisdom. Wisdom, much like water, retains the form of the container it occupies, and though it has a multitude of purposes, its most important one is to help us survive. Treat this book like water; you can swim in it, soak in it, bathe in it, cook with it, use it to grow things, and even clean things, but if you did all of those things and never drank any, you would surely die. Make sure you drink as much of this information as needed, and make sure your neighbor gets plenty of it as well. This is the type of information that truly needs to become a part of you, so reread it at least 5 times in order to make it secondary knowledge that flows effortlessly from you. If you feel there are some things in this book you need to revisit, I encourage you by all means, open up to the chapter you need and refresh yourself.

With all the books in the world, I now have much more of an understanding of the sacrificial lifestyle and countless hours, events, pleasures and family time it costs to bring forth those amazing pieces of work. I greatly appreciate the many authors who have come before me, and dedicated their wisdom to bettering the lives of the people they share the world with. It has been my pleasure to offer you some insight into your journey in business and in dating. Being a boss means you have the power to change the things you want to change, and the insight to know what you need to accept. Creating the life you want and obtaining the rewards you desire will require making tough decisions, but with each sacrifice you're willing to make toward your happiness you are reminding yourself that although being a boss is not easy, it's who you're called to be.

Until we meet again, adios!

J.T. Boyd was born and raised in North Carolina. He moved to Los Angeles after losing his job just before his 30th birthday. He found his footing helping to grow startups, and is currently the CFO of a fast-growing non-profit organization in Southern California. He is married with 2 children.

J.T. Boyd has many times experienced firsthand the challenges of creating and being a part of something new, both in business and in dating. Despite some failures along the way, they have all led to his many successes. He specializes in leadership, business and relationship consulting. He is also a certified life coach and the founder of Good Boyd Group.

Visit him online at www.jtboyd.co.

Made in the USA
Las Vegas, NV
26 September 2023

78165792R00132